D0120921

Towards
A Renewed Priesthood

To Jennifer, Simon and Jonathan,
for their faithfulness, patience,
understanding and support.

Prayer of St Benedict

Gracious and Holy Father,
Please give me:
intellect to understand you,
reason to discern you,
diligence to seek you,
wisdom to find you,
a heart to meditate upon you
ears to hear you
eyes to see you,
a tongue to proclaim you,
a way of life pleasing to you,
patience to wait for you
and perseverance to look for you.
Grant me a perfect end—
your holy presence,
a blessed resurrection
and life everlasting.

Towards
A Renewed Priesthood

Arthur Middleton

With my good wishes

Arthur Middleton

Gracewing

First published in 1995

Gracewing
Fowler Wright Books
2 Southern Ave, Leominster
Herefordshire HR6 0QF

Gracewing books are distributed

In New Zealand by
Catholic Supplies Ltd
80 Adelaide Road
Wellington
New Zealand

In Australia by
Charles Paine Pty Ltd
8 Ferris Street
North Parramatta
NSW 2151, Australia

In USA by
Morehouse Publishing
PO Box 1321
Harrisburg
PA 17105
USA

In Canada by
Meakin and Associates
Unit 17, 81 Aurega Drive
Nepean, Ontario
KZE 7Y5, Canada

All rights reserved. No part of this publication may be reproduced, stored in a retrieval system, or transmitted in any form, or by any means, electronic, mechanical, photocopying, recording, or otherwise, without the written permission of the publisher.

© Arthur Middleton 1995
Cover illustration by Gill Onions

ISBN 0 85244 273 4

Typesetting by Reesprint, Radley, Oxfordshire, OX14 3AJ

Printed at Redwood Books, Trowbridge, Wiltshire.

Contents

Preface

The substance of what is written in this book is the fruit of thirty years living as a priest, but it is also a vision of priesthood that has been handed on to me by numerous priests, living and departed, who, in the course of my life have been an inspiration and guide; some from early childhood, others in training; numerous priests not only from within the Anglican Communion, but also from other churches, with whom I have had close fellowship in study and ministry. To these priests I express my warm appreciation and thanks. I would like also to thank my son Simon, who proof-read the manuscript and made some useful corrections and suggestions.

The opportunity to reflect on what a priest is has come to me through invitations to assist and help other clergy. I am grateful for the invitations from various Deaneries in the Durham, Newcastle Dioceses and beyond to visit Chapter Meetings and deliver Papers, conduct Quiet Days and Study Days, and with them reflect on the nature of priesthood and how it is to be lived in the world today.

Parts of this book have been circulated privately by request. Chapter 5 was published substantially in its present form in *Mount Carmel*[1] under the title 'Priesthood and Contemplative Life'. Chapter 6 contains the substance of an article in the same journal[2] under the title 'Towards a Living Christian Spirituality'. They were subsequently republished in Australia in a booklet *For Their Sakes* edited by the Revd Kevin Joyner.

In a time of such confusion we need to return to the sources of life and rediscover our roots, not in mere thought, but in the life in which we live, the mystical and sacramental life that reaches beyond the intellectual into the realm of imagination, intuition or wholeness, and is by way of liturgy, prayer and spirituality. Here we shall find that the rule for the renewal of the Church will be the rule for the renewal of ourselves in priesthood and life.

Notes

1. *A Quarterly Review of the Spiritual Life*, Vol. 29 No. 1 Spring 1981.
2. *Ibid.*, Vol. 24 No. 1 Spring 1976.

1

From Despondency to Conversion

Despondency about Ourselves

In 1845, in the wake of Newman's secession to Rome, Dr
Pusey wrote to Samuel Wilberforce the Bishop-elect of
Oxford summarizing the position in these words: 'As far as
I can see, what is chiefly at work is not attraction towards
Rome, but despondency about ourselves.'[1] To the task of
reassurance, the new bishop was called. Despondency about
ourselves, but for quite different reasons, describes what
many priests have experienced in recent years. The causes
are various and will differ in detail from one individual to
another, but two underlying influences have affected priests
most. First, a similar situation to that described by Bishop
Butler in his *Primary Charge to the Durham Clergy*, 'the
general decay of religion in this nation; which is now
observed by everyone, and has been the complaint of all
serious persons... the number of those... who profess themselves unbelievers increases, and with their numbers their
zeal.'[2] Secondly, the gradual growth and development of a
kind of thinking that reduces the priest to a mere *functionary*, that sees him and evaluates him as a professional person
who possesses skills and techniques to be acquired through
training. Once trained he is then to be concerned with using
and allocating his skills and techniques in as efficient a way
as possible. Management replaces ministry, in order to allow
efficiency, planning, and the use of resources to become the
central determining factors in the shaping of mission. The
priest becomes the administrative functionary or leader, and

administration rather than doctrine determines the form which the Church takes.

It is another side of a kind of secular determinism that dominates contemporary ecclesiastical circles. Kenneth Leech is critical of its impact on pastoral ministry and cites Urban Holmes who wrote in *The Future Shape of the Ministry*, that such thinking excludes the rôles of prayer and sacrament, or assigns them to a very low status. Their value lies in a utilitarian function, as means to achieve some other end, ways to help us do something else better.[3] As far back as 1916, Neville Figgis saw this creeping secularisation, rather than idleness, as the principal danger facing the Church. Preaching in Salisbury Cathedral on Trinity Sunday 1916, he pointed out that the evil of the Church is:

> ... the doing of Church work in a spirit of mere business, something to be got through. The only way to avoid this is for the priest to be instant in prayer. If he does not he will lose that touch of the supernatural without which he has no right to be a priest at all.[4]

Alongside this problem of increasing functionalism, there is also a crisis of authority. This state of crisis is particularly acute within the Anglican Communion, but is also present throughout the Christian world. It finds expression in the doubt and unreliability that is now attributed to foundation doctrine in Scripture and Creed, and in the sources on which they depend. Writing in *The Times*,[5] the former Anglican Bishop and newly ordained Roman Catholic priest Graham Leonard wrote:

> On the one side there are those who believe that the Christian gospel is revealed by God at a time and in a place of his choosing, through events which are of significance for all time and for all generations. They believe that it is the duty of the Church, under the judgement of the gospel, to discern how it is to be expressed in different times and cultures. On the other side are those who believe that the gospel should be adapted to the cultural and intellectual attitudes and demands of successive generations.

He quotes from an *Open Synod Newsletter* in which it is claimed that the wisdom of the past, Scripture or Tradition, are merely one source among many insights, and authoritative answers to any questions are suspect since the only authority is 'the tentative response of the individual disciple's conscience.' Such a view does not reflect the principle and spirit of the New Testament, and is a product of an increasing culture of relativism.

Fr Leonard goes on to explore the problems arising from this. First, the assumption that people of the *Tradition* are negative and uncreative in rigidly applying doctrine to contemporary needs. Yet the history of the Church proves otherwise, in that she has only proved her relevancy to any age, when she has been faithful to the eternal gospel. Her failures have always occurred when she has been:

> ... locked in the attitudes and thought-forms of a particular generation (as for example in Europe in the eighteenth century, when the so-called Enlightenment dismissed revelation, leaving only the reason of man as the touchstone for all human knowledge and behaviour).

The second problem arises from a pervasive liberalism that has infiltrated all traditions, leaving a confusion which affects the credibility of the Church itself. The third problem is the content of the Church's gospel. Doctrine which is necessary to salvation is embodied for the Church of England in her *Formularies* and *The Book of Common Prayer*. These are an expression of such doctrine. Yet so often it is precisely these doctrines so necessary for salvation that are being denied the hungry sheep. One can sniff a pervasive and contemporary Arianism behind the policies and innovations that are being thrust upon the Church, and like the Arianism of old, it merely reflects contemporary fashion.

In *The Other Side of 1984*, Leslie Newbigin has written that we have come to the end of Renaissance man. He writes:

... if the immense achievements of autonomous reason seem to have produced a world which is at best meaningless and at worst full of demons, then it could be that Polanyi is right, that we shall not find renewal within the framework of the assumptions which the men of the Enlightenment held to be 'self-evident', that there is needed a radical conversion, a new starting point which begins as an act of trust in divine grace as something simply given to be received in faith and gratitude.

What is written here starts from this conviction that such a new starting-point is crucial to the credibility and life of the Church, and that a radical conversion is most urgently needed within the priesthood. The nineteenth Sunday after Pentecost in the *ASB* reminds us that faith is a free gift of God to those who seek it in true poverty of spirit. As in the case of Abraham, the gift of faith will be for the priest the beginning of his spiritual and intellectual journey and not the end. A beginning in which God's transformation will make all things new in the justification of that faith, and where the starting point must be the rejection of that liberal secularist reversal of this essential Christian assumption of faith.

The Character of Priesthood

Julian of Norwich is an important female mystic who offers hope in the midst of death, despair and destruction. In her essay on this theme,[7] Anna Maria Reynolds CP, quotes Bernard Haring's depiction of a 'Universal Congress of Skunks', presided over by the Supervisor of Devils, the Super-Skunk. The main item on the agenda is the formulation of a strategy for the transformation of the Church our enemy into a perfect sacrament of pessimism. Let Christians get away with anything so long as they destroy hope. Returning from India in 1974 after nearly 40 years, Leslie Newbigin commented on the lack of hope in this country, contrasting it with India where belief in a better future flourished even in the midst of some atrocious conditions.[8] Julian's hope rested on something outside herself.

The remedy is that our Lord is with us, keeping us and leading us into the fullness of joy; for our Lord intends this to be an endless joy, that he who will be our bliss when we are there [heaven] will be our protector while we are here, our way and our heaven in true love and trust.[9]

In his *Enthronement Sermon* as Bishop of Durham, Bishop Lightfoot said of Bishop Butler, '... there accompanied him in his passage to eternity' what 'had dominated his life in time', 'a consciousness of an eternal presence'. In Lightfoot's last charge to the clergy of Durham, he urged the 'yielding of ourselves up to the full influence of the Divine Presence' and to 'endeavour to raise up in the hearts of their people such a sense of God, as shall be an habitual ready principle of reverence, love, gratitude, hope, trust... and obedience.' Here the priest is seen as more than a mere *functionary*, but the one to whom is entrusted the spiritual guidance of the people in his charge, God's people who are gathered to give themselves to the collective quest for God. He has become responsible for them and will make his mark on them, but the formation he gives them will be in accordance with the pattern of his own spiritual life. The priest is more than a leader of the local church. He is its teacher and guide. His rôle is not to impart mere cerebral knowledge in a classroom idiom, but to *edify*, and *build-up* members of the Body of Christ, disclosing to them of that which happened when they were born again through water and Spirit. He is to introduce people into the life of the Church, to unfold its meaning, its contents and purpose, that they might taste and see how good the Lord is. First taste, then understand. Our concern as priests is to edify them in the knowledge and love of God, devoting our lives to helping them grow in the divine likeness. The Pastoral Prayer of Aelred of Rievaulx might well become ours:

> My will is that all your gifts to me be
> at their disposal absolutely. I will
> spend myself unreservedly on their behalf;
> all that I am, my life, my views,
> understanding, all be at their service.[10]

The priest has the difficult and arduous duty of adapting himself to different temperaments, accommodating himself to the character, ways, disposition, gifts, and shortcomings of each; doing as circumstances demand and as God wants doing.

> But the whole of our treatment and exertion is concerned with the hidden man of the heart, and our warfare is directed against that adversary and foe within us, who uses ourselves as his weapons against ourselves, and most fearful of all hands us over to the death of sin. In opposition to these foes we are in need of great and perfect faith, of still greater co-operation on the part of God, and, as I am persuaded, of no slight counter-manœuvring on our own part, which must manifest itself both in word and deed, if ourselves, the most precious possession we have, are to be duly tended and cleansed and made as deserving as possible.[11]

Gregory of Nazianzen goes on to say that the scope of our art is:

> ... to provide the soul with wings, to rescue it from the world and give it to God, and to watch over that which is in His Image, if it abides, to take it by the hand, if it is in danger, to restore it, if ruined, to make Christ dwell in the heart by the Spirit, and in short to deify, and bestow heavenly bliss upon, one who belongs to the heavenly host.[12]

This is the character of God's ministry which has a continuity from the Law and the prophets to Christ the incarnate God, who in his death and resurrection healed our weakness, restoring the Old Adam to the place from which he fell and conducted us to the *Tree of Life* from which the *Tree of Knowledge* estranged us. Of this ministry of healing, we who are set over others are the ministers and fellow-labourers. The implication for someone entering into such a ministry is what Gregory himself wrote about at a time when many were clamouring to be priests for the wrong motives.

> A man must himself be cleansed before cleansing others; himself become wise that he may make others wise; become

light before he can give light; draw near to God before he can bring others near; be hallowed before he can hallow them; be possessed of hands before leading others by the hand and wisdom before he can speak wisely.[13]

The government of souls is therefore an art, which Nazianzen's namesake Gregory the Great takes up in his *Pastoral Rule*. In comparing it to the art of medicine they both draw out what they mean by this. As the formation of the medical system and the doctor's rôle within it is impossible to understand in terms of a mere theoretical understanding of care and skill, but needs experience and practice, so must this be required of the pastor of souls who is practising what Gregory the Great calls the art of arts. Therefore, says Gregory Nazianzen:

> Just as it is not safe for those who walk on a lofty tightrope to lean to either side, for even though the inclination seems slight, it has no slight consequences, but their safety depends on their perfect balance: so in the case of each one of us, if he leans to either side, whether from vice or ignorance, no slight danger of a fall into sin is incurred, both for himself and those who are led by him. But we really walk in the King's highway, and take care not to turn aside from it either to the right hand or to the left, as the Proverbs say. For such is the case with our passions and such in this matter is the task of the Good Shepherd, if he is to know properly the souls of his flock, and to guide them according to the methods of a pastoral care which is right and just, and worthy of our true Shepherd.[14]

An Ecclesial Christology

Walking in the *King's Highway* is a particular orientation of Christian living that calls for special emphasis in today's Church. Our rule for the renewal of the Church will be the rule for the renewal of our lives as priests and pastors. Its starting point must be the overcoming of our difficulty when attempting to assimilate ourselves into him who is our point of reference and departure and in whom we live.

The crisis of church life is based in the final analysis not on the difficulties of adaptation with regard to life today, but on the difficulties with regard to him in whom our faith has its roots, and from whose being it draws its heights and its depths, its way and its future, Jesus Christ and his message of the Kingdom of God.[15]

Too often we try to adapt him to ourselves.

To think in this way—to think of following and imitating Christ—is not to adopt a bourgeois liberal theology that takes him as a mere model. Mere imitation of Christ is not enough. Crucifixion with Christ, re-creation and transfiguration into Christ-likeness by participation in the divine nature. The rebirth into a new dimension not previously known. This is the requirement and our goal. This is what St Paul means by re-presenting Christ, and is further emphasized by Our Lord himself, who repeatedly forced all those whom he called to follow him, to abandon their previous mode of existence. The demands he made were not just aimed at changing attitudes. They were intended to cause a fundamental movement, an absorption into the *New Life* which is salvation and which is Christ. The radical acceptance of a new life and direction that was no longer confined to the mental disposition of those who followed him. Today, the weakness of the Church lies in its reduction of its mission to the dissemination of Christian attitudes. This merely objectifies these beliefs and detaches them from their real context in life, as ways of thinking which are the natural corollary of living in a certain kind of way. The attempt is then made to impress these beliefs upon people who are not living a life which incorporates them. Even if successful this will only dispose them mentally rather than existentially. Is not this the inherent weakness of what is called influencing the structures?

It is incumbent upon us as priests and pastors to go back to our roots and discover to what extent the imperatives of following Christ in *love, obedience, sacrifice, freedom, joy,* and *poverty,* can affect the pattern of our lives and the pastoral contexts in which we minister. We need to discover the extent to which this following of Christ can send the Church along pathways that today it is hardly thought capable of following any longer. To rediscover the Church in this way will be the most decisive aspect of a new spiritual realism, when it is again realized that the Church is not just a company of believers, but the Body of Christ. This is the rediscovery of a deeper dimension, a rediscovery of the Divine Redeemer in our midst, among his faithful flock. As George Florovsky wrote:

> It is already recognized by many, that the true solution to all social problems lies somehow in the reconstruction of the Church. In a time such as this, one has to preach the 'whole Christ', Christ and the Church—*totus Christus, caput et corpus.*'[16]

This is what is meant by an *ecclesial Christology*. The technical theological term Christology is well known, but too often has been confined to a mere theoretical understanding of Christ concerning the balance and relationship between the divinity and humanity, defined by such terms as Nestorian, Monophysite, Arian, Docetist or Chalcedonian. The need is to extend the term Christology and include within its meaning Biology, Archaeology, and Geology. These disciplines embrace within their meaning the practice of the science of which one has a theoretical or intellectual understanding. To dispense with the *ecclesial* dimension is akin to the chemist dispensing with his laboratory.

An *ecclesial Christology* implies that Christ is not only to be worshipped, but that he is also to be seen as a way along which we can travel. Every attempt to understand him implies a journey or a following. Only by following him and allowing ourselves to be transfigured into his likeness can we know him with whom we are dealing. Christological knowledge is formed and transferred, not primarily through mere conceptual statements, but in accounts of following Christ which express the lived experience of the practical Christology. In a nation characterized by a general decay in religion and an apathy and indifference towards the things of

God, these accounts are vital to the Church's witness.

> A Church marked by the following of Christ, will be saved
> from the instinctive fear, that meets every crisis by organizing
> itself into an administration, that wants to meet the difficulties
> by raising the organizational and structural level of the
> Church's resources.[17]

The Structure of Following Christ

The structure of following Christ is in part mystical, and in
part grounded in a concrete situation. The mystical aspect of
following Christ never operates in a vacuum, it cannot be an
esoteric adventure in isolation from its social context. As
Metz points out, when the double mystical and situational
composition of following Christ is ignored we end up with
a half-truth, and the following of Christ ends up exemplify-
ing only half the truth of what is involved. The result is
either the reduction of the following of Christ to a purely
social and political dimension of behaviour, or its degener-
ation into a private spirituality—a kind of dead pietism.

To say that our following of Christ has a mystical compo-
nent is to say that our life is under the direction of Christ
and involves something more than mere mental speculation.
It calls for a disposition of soul—a love and desire for Christ
in whose way we follow. Knowledge, if it is to be real
knowledge, must lead on to personal commitment, for
knowledge supposes likeness. To know is in some sense to
become the thing known while remaining oneself. Doctrine
then becomes concrete in character, in that it deals less with
objective and impersonal speculation than with bearing
witness to an experience. In it the things of the Spirit are
described as they have been lived by those who have
encountered them, perceived them, tasted them; not in a
sensible way, but spiritually, by having been affected by
them. A living Christian teaching must of necessity have
been lived, must take its direction from life, and be directed
to life. Such teaching will hold out an invitation to share that

experience and be a call to personal commitment, because it brings a person in the depths of his soul face to face with realities that intimately concern him. In order to understand any teaching, any doctrine, a person must conform his life to it. This entails that he put himself in accord with the spirituality he is considering.

While it is personal, Christian formation is never individualistic, and must centre on the whole person as a member of a community—the Church. The mystical needs the situational, the parish or worshipping community, in which the following of Christ is articulated in concrete ways. A priest, a Christian, forms part of a community that offers him help and requires him to act in a community spirit. His neighbour must always be included in the following of Christ. It is lived out as a body—as the people in the community of salvation—in the awareness of others at our side, united in the same spiritual purpose and making for the solidarity of the people of God.

Within the community of the Church, priest and people share in the common task of following Christ. Like the holy tent that was Yahweh's dwelling place and which was moved about with the Chosen People, the local Church is journeying with God in Christ, and is the company with whom we journey through life. Here is the setting of our spiritual experiences, the *milieu* in which our following of Christ takes place, the microcosm of the larger Church. It recalls us to the essential nature of the Christian life, that each of us is an instrument for the sanctification of each other, and that our unity and peace as the people of God is realized in and through Christ in whose way we follow.

The Challenge to the Priest

The new and sharp perspective that the Church of today needs can never be the fruit of some special kind of speculation. Rather it must be the fruit of a deeply lived experience of the mystery of Christ. It is the call to holiness, to God-centred living, which is not anti-world but Kingdom-centred. Response to such a call will require a spirit of penitence in which will grow a discernment and perception of sin. This will not develop by way of debate, but through following the way of the Cross in sacrifice and obedience as one responds to the concrete realities of living. True holiness ensures that human growth and spiritual growth are never separated, and that there is always compassion and forgiveness for the sinner, but never the condoning of sin.

The implication of this for the pastor of souls to whom is entrusted the spiritual guidance of the Christian community will be obvious. He can only form it in accordance with the pattern of his own spiritual life. His spiritual life cannot be a private segment of life divorced from social and political concerns, but must be an overall direction of life towards God and his Kingdom. His devotional life will be a way of speaking about his whole life orientated towards God.

> It stands for the total orientation of life towards God... it is real in its own right, an action transcending and embracing all the separate souls taking part in it. The individual as such dies to his own separate selfhood on entering the Divine Society.[18]

The discipline required is nothing less than that whereby a man's faith becomes the subject of his much praying and the object of his much thinking. Praying and thinking, *the Kingdom of Love* and *the Kingdom of Knowledge* can never be separated. It is within such discipline that faith itself becomes a possession held with such firmness, clarity and coherence, as hard study, sincere prayer, and deeper than normal thinking can ensure. Our search is for an ever-renewed and renewing realization of God and an intuitive grasp of the Gospel of God *who is always more ready to hear than we to pray and is wont to give more than either we desire or deserve*. God constantly takes the initiative. Paul bears this out when he tells the Philippians how he had been apprehended by God in Christ, rather than he himself having apprehended Christ.

It is indeed nothing less than the challenge to conversion and new life, which brings us back to some words of Gregory Nazianzen:

> ... no-one is worthy of the mightiness of God, and the sacrifice, and the priesthood, who has not first presented himself to God, a living, holy sacrifice, and set forth the reasonable well-pleasing service and sacrificed to God the sacrifice of praise and the contrite spirit, which is the only sacrifice required of us by the Giver of all; how could I dare to offer to him the external sacrifice, the antitype of the great mysteries, or clothe myself with the garb and name of priest, before my hands had been consecrated by holy works; before my eyes had been accustomed to gaze safely upon created things, with wonder for the Creator and without injury to the creature; before my ear had been sufficiently opened to the instruction of the Lord, and he opened my ear to hear... a wise man's word in an obedient ear; before my mouth had been opened to draw in the Spirit, and opened wide to be filled with the spirit of speaking mysteries and doctrines; and my lips bound, to use the words of wisdom by divine knowledge... before my feet had been set upon the rock... and my footsteps directed in Godly fashion....[19]

The illumination that Gregory sees as the prime necessity of the priest, comes when like him the priest begins with himself and investigates the possibilities of conversion and new life. Such a possibility can come only through the direct action of the living God by whom Saul of Tarsus was apprehended and became alive, not merely to live a new life in an exclusively ethical sense, though that was a consequence. Saul's awakening and conversion went much further. It gave him an understanding of God fuller and richer than he had ever hitherto conceived. It had a theological consequence, which, because he is so recognized by God, and himself recognizes God, he becomes in a completely deep sense Paul the Theologian. No-one can become a theologian except in this way, nor will any priest see the pregnant fecund theological problems clearly other than through the very fullness of insight which God himself initiates. Our

moment of illumination is born when we offer our whole
being to knowing the truth which is beyond concepts and
then receive it as a converting and transfiguring experience.

Notes

1.   G.W. Daniel, *Bishop Wilberforce,* (Methuen, London 1905).
2.   Bp Butler, 'A Charge delivered to the Clergy, 1751' *Works,*
       ed. Gladstone (Clarendon, Oxford 1897), p. 334.
3.   Kenneth Leech, 'The Pastor and his Devotional Life', *Exposi-
       tory Times,* Vol. 91 No.12 September 1980, p. 356.
4.   'The Office of a Priest', *Defects in English Religion* (Scott,
       London 1917) p. 60.
5.   *The Times* 15 June 1990.
6.   Leslie Newbigin, *The Other Side of 1984,* (WCC 1985), p. 26.
7.   Robert Llewellyn (ed.), *Julian, Woman of our Day* (DLT
       1985), p. 11.
8.   Newbigin, *ibid.* p. 1.
9.   *Julian of Norwich, Revelations of Divine Love,* ed. Clifton
       Wolters, (Penguin Books, 1978) ch. 77, p. 200.
10.   'Oratio Pastoralis', ed. C. Dumont, *Sources Chretiennes* No.
       76.7, cited by Hallier, *The Monastic Theology of Aelred of
       Rievaulx,* p. 294.
11.   Gregory of Nazianzen, Oration 2, 'In Defence of his Flight to
       Pontus', *The Nicene and Post-Nicene Fathers,* 2nd Series,
       Vol. VII, 21 p. 209.
12.   Nazianzen, *ibid.* 22, p. 209.
13.   Nazianzen, *ibid.* 71, p. 219.
14.   Nazianzen, *ibid.* 34, p. 211.
15.   *Our Hope: A Confession of Faith for our Time;* The German
       RC Synod of Bishops, cited by Johannes Metz, *Followers
       of Christ, The Religious Life and the Church,* trans.
       Thomas Linton (Burns & Oates/Paulist Press 1978), p. 33.
16.   George Florovsky, *Bible, Church and Tradition: An Eastern
       Orthodox View,* (Nordland 1972) p. 16.
17.   Metz, *ibid.* p. 32, to whom I am indebted for some insights I
       have developed in my own way.
18.   Evelyn Underhill, *Worship* (Nisbet 1958), pp. 84, 86.
19.   Nazianzen, *ibid.,* 95 p. 223–224.

2

George Herbert and the Priest Today

A Living Example

Living examples of great ideals are always an inspiration, a mirror into which we can look for correctives to our own image. Coming into contact with them can be a converting experience, and one which can quite literally change the course of our lives. The purpose of this chapter is to rest awhile in the presence of George Herbert, that the spirit of priesthood living in him might begin to affect us in that kind of way. George Herbert was only forty when he died and had been a priest for only three years, the length of what is technically called serving one's title, though he had been a deacon for some years before. Nevertheless, thinking back to that time in one's own ministry will for most priests, only emphasize the greatness of Herbert's achievement. Although the manner of life has changed considerably since his time, the principle and spirit in which he lived and ministered as a priest have remained an inspiration and model for succeeding generations of Anglican clergy. The parish to which he was sent, the united benefice of Fulston St Peter with Bemerton St Andrew was far from being a plumb living, having dilapidated and drab buildings with little income. Yet Walton[1] records that when, at his Induction, he was shut into Bemerton church and left alone to toll the bell (the custom at Institutions in those days), he stayed much longer than normal. A friend looking through the window saw him prostrate before the Altar, at which moment as he told his friend Mr Woodnot, he set himself some rules for the future management of his life, and there and then made a vow to keep them. Four years earlier when he told a friend at court of his intention to seek ordination, and the friend's response was that such a life was unbecoming of one so nobly born and endowed with such intellectual gifts, Herbert replied:

> It hath been formerly judged that the Domestick Servants of the King of Heaven, should be of the noblest Families on Earth: and, though the Iniquity of the late Times have made Clergy-men meanly valued, and the sacred name of PRIEST contemptible; yet I will labour to make it honourable, by consecrating all my learning, and all my poor abilities, to advance the glory of that God that gave them; knowing, that I can never do too much for him, that hath done so much for me, as to make me a Christian. And I will labour to be like my Saviour, by making Humility lovely in the eyes of all men, and by following the merciful and meek example of my dear Jesus.[2]

On the same night of his Induction he said to Mr Woodnot:

> I now look back upon my aspiring thoughts and think myself more happy than if I had attain'd what then I so ambitiously thirsted for: And I can now behold the Court with an impartial Eye, and see plainly, that it is made up of Fraud, and Title, and Flattery, and many other such empty, imaginary and painted pleasures: Pleasures that are so empty, as not to satisfy when they are enjoy'd; but in God and his service, is a fullness of all joy and pleasure, and no satiety: And I will now use all my endeavours to bring my Relations and Dependants to a love and relyance on him, who never fails those that trust him. *But above all, I will be sure to live well, because the vertuous life of a Clergyman, is the most powerful eloquence to persuade all that see it, to reverence and love, and at least, to desire to live like him. And this I will do, because I know we live in an Age that hath more need of good examples, than precepts...*

Herbert continued saying that he would beseech God who had honoured him so much to call him to serve at his Altar, and by his special grace had put into his heart these good desires and resolutions, that by the same grace he would give him the ghostly strength to bring them to good effect. All this would be done as to bring glory to 'my JESUS, whom I have this day taken to be my Master and Governour; and I am so proud of his service, that I will always observe, and obey, and do his Will....'[3]

From Public Orator of the University of Cambridge and Fellow of Trinity College and an influential figure in the Royal Court, he becomes a model parish priest whose life is as powerful as his words. Walton says that it deserved the eloquence of a Chrysostom to commend and declare it, and this is no romantic exaggeration. Nicholas Ferrar, whose Little Gidding Community must have influenced Herbert, wrote in the 1633 Preface to *The Temple*, that Herbert's life in the faithful discharge of his ministry was such as to make him justly a companion of the primitive saints. His own brother, a person not renowned for exaggeration, claimed that his life was so holy and exemplary that around Salisbury he was *little less than sainted*.[4] This does not mean that he was an ineffective introvert, for there were many practical concerns to which he had to turn his mind including the repair of dilapidated buildings. Furthermore, he was an immensely attractive, cheerful, human and friendly person with a facility for mixing socially.

The Country Parson

Among Herbert's friends were the Caroline divines, Lancelot Andrewes, Francis Bacon, William Laud, John Donne and Nicholas Ferrar; men concerned to maintain the catholic integrity of the Church of England as primitive, rather than papal. Like Lancelot Andrewes' *Private Devotions*, Herbert's *The Country Parson*, was drawn up for private use rather than for publication. In it he set down the rules that should govern the discipline of prayer, study, preaching, visiting the sick, his conversations, recreation and the priest's relationship with his churchwardens and people; principles he had laid down for himself at his Induction and which were later expanded in the light of experience. It expresses the spirit of his self-oblation, familiar to any priest concerned to serve Christ fully, for the fruitfulness of a priest's ministry is directly related to the degree of his own self-oblation and may not manifest itself until it is a harvest reaped by his successor. *The Country Parson* expresses Herbert's under-standing of the nature of priesthood. He sees the priest as being Christ's deputy, literally a vicar, dedicated to the winning of people back to the obedience of God. The dignity of a priest lies in 'that a priest may do that which Christ did, and by his authority, and as his vicegerent; the duty, in that a priest is to do that which Christ did, and after his manner, both for doctrine and life.'[5] Priesthood was not a convenient and historically conditioned form of Church organization, but rooted in the Incarnation—in the priesthood and mission of Christ himself. His view of priesthood was ontological or non-functionalist; priesthood being determined by what a priest is, rather than by what he does. He is a priest for ever and does not cease to be a priest merely because he cannot carry out his priestly ministry.

It was a time when many people were disillusioned with the clergy, and in a sea of Calvinism and Puritanism others were questioning its theological foundations. Herbert belonged unmistakeably to that school of Hooker, Andrewes and Laud, among whom were many fine priests mentioned in the following chapter, such as Henry Hammond, Herbert Thorndike and John Cosin. Men whose ministries resisted the replacement of the catholic priesthood in the Church of England by a presbyterian model of ministry. It was the convictions, faithfulness and dedication of such priests that saved the Anglican priesthood from dissolution. Herbert was one of such men; men who by their own example were re-asserting these theological foundations, admitting at the same time that people had lost sight of the ideal through a shortage of living examples. Many country clergy were liable to gross immorality, drinking, swearing and brawling.

In another of his Salisbury walks, Herbert met with a neighbour Minister, and after some friendly Discourse betwixt
them, and some condolement for the decay of Piety, and too
general contempt of the Clergy, he took occasion to say: 'One
cure for these distempers would be for the Clergy themselves
to keep the Ember-Weeks—strictly, and beg their Parishioners
to joyn with them in Fasting and Prayers, for a more Religious Clergy.

'And another cure would be, for themselves to restore the
great and neglected duty of Catechising, on which the salvation of so many of the poor and ignorant Laypeople does
depend; but principally, that the Clergy themselves would be
sure to live unblameably; and that the dignifi'd Clergy
especially... would... take all occasions to express a visible
humility and charity in their lives; for this would force a love
and imitation, and an unfeigned reverence from all that knew
them to be such.... This... would be a cure for the wickedness
and growing Atheism of our Age. And, my dear Brother, till
this be done by us, and done in earnest, let no man expect a
reformation of the manners of the Laity: for 'tis not learning,
but this, this only, that must do it; and till then, the fault must
lye at our doors.'[6]

Herbert saw an ontological difference—a difference in
essence—between ministerial priesthood and the priesthood
of the people of God as a whole. Ministerial priesthood was
not superior, but ontologically inferior to the priesthood of
the laity. What superiority it had, it gained by its superior
exercise of humility and by its ability to emulate the ministry
of Christ. Herbert's life as a priest was an integration of
prayer, study, teaching and pastoral care, embodying his
understanding of the priest as a man of God, a teacher and
pastor.

The Man of God

The duty and the dignity of the priest already quoted,
illustrate Herbert's understanding of priesthood as more than
mere external resemblance to Christ. It is to be in the
Pauline sense a putting-on of Christ. An interior conformity

to the mysteries celebrated, an interior likeness that issues from a willingness to be crucified with Christ. In Chapter 1, St Paul is quoted in the first chapter of his *Letter to the Colossians* as one who 'plainly avoucheth, that he fills up that which is behind of the afflictions of Christ in his flesh, for his body's sake, which is the Church: wherein is contained the complete definition of a minister'.[7] There is an integrity between the sufferings he is willing to endure for the sake of the Church in his daily life and his actions in celebrating the Eucharist wherein he sees the priest taking on more fully the likeness of Christ. In the spirit of Chrysostom he sees his daily life as a priest, distributed in the same way as Christ distributes himself at the Eucharist. To know the things of God requires a personal acquaintance that can only come through a deep interior life of prayer, that weds doctrine and life in one. Only when such a marriage has taken place in the priest, will his preaching be effective. In his poem *The Windows*, he echoes this insight where he speaks:

> Lord, how can man preach thy eternall word?

> To be a window, through thy grace,

> Making thy life to shine within
> Thy holy Preachers...

> Doctrine and life, colours and light, in one
> When they combine and mingle, bring
> A strong regard and awe: but speech alone
> Doth vanish like a flaring thing,
> And in the eare, not conscience ring.

Similarly his poem *Teach Me, My God and King*, speaks of *In all things thee to see*, and in such a consciousness of God's presence discovering that it makes even drudgery divine. The poem *Prayer*, speaks of it as:

God's breath in man returning to his birth,
The soul in paraphrase, heart in
pilgrimage,
The Christian plummet sounding heav'n
and earth;
and of, Heaven in the ordinarie....

These insights illustrate his understanding of praycr as contemplative, as well as his belief that such prayer is to be the normal vocation of a priest. Here is no escapist prayer, but the mingling of contemplation in a world of action in which eternity graces time. Only through such prayer will we recognize the Creator in his Creation—the evidence of *heaven* in the ordinary things of earth—and be more able to participate deeply in the pain and pleasure of lifc. This is the case because through contemplative vision we shall have a more enlightened understanding of its problems. Such transfiguration comes only through the way of Christ in Crucifixion and Resurrection; through the death which is the way to life. For Herbert, the priest must tread this road if he is to share the joys and sorrows of his people, agonize with them in their problems, confusions and hopes and identify with them in their life and work while remaining in God. Yet he cannot do this if there is no discipline of prayer. Herbert was diligent in saying the Daily Office at 10.00 a.m. and 4.00 p.m. every day, ringing the bell beforehand. Walton tells us that workers in the fields on hearing the bell would stop and pray. One of his hymns echoes this prayer, 'Seven whole days, not one in seven, I will praise thee'; this is nothing less than a whole life orientated to God in prayer, where his ministry was continually laid before God to be purified and redeemed, that he might be taught, 'In all things thee to see'.

The Priest as Teacher

We have already mentioned some of the great priests of the Caroline era. These were men of massive learning, and

Herbert was no exception to such learning. However such
learning was not mere isolated knowledge, it was all part of
his offering to God, consecrated to his service. Herbert was
not a priest who moaned about his gifts not being used by
the Church, or about his being in a place where his gifts
would not be used to the full or be appreciated. There was
none of this kind of self-regarding in Herbert. He believed
that any priest worthy of his title would find ways of using
his gifts in God's service, and this he did and expected any
other priest to do the same. To find in men of learning a
humility equal to it, is to find a person who never loses the
disposition of the student, and this should be the mark of
every priest. Herbert's concern was that a priest should have
a knowledge of the knowledge of his people, that he should
know what was required of them in their daily work, in
order that he might lead them to a knowledge of the things
of God. In this sense not only is the priest the teacher of the
congregation, they in their turn are his teachers.

However there is a certain kind of knowledge that is
essential to a priest if he is to do his daily work, and if his
learning is to carry practical implications. His primary source
of knowledge must be Holy Scripture, wherein are precepts
to live by, doctrines for knowledge, examples to follow and
promises for comfort. He writes in one of his poems:

> ... let my heart
> Suck ev'ry letter, and a honey gain,
> .... [The Holy Scriptures]

The prerequisite to a proper understanding of Scripture was
a holy life, the conforming of one's life to the doctrine.
No-one can understand Scripture unless he or she is seeking
to practise what is read there, 'because they are not understood but with the same Spirit that writ them.'[8] The second
means is prayer. One should begin reading with a prayer that
God may open one's eyes to this supernatural knowledge. A
third means is the collation of Scripture with Scripture,
recognizing that there is a unity and that the self-same Spirit
is at work throughout, and the comparing of any text with

the coherence found. The fourth method recommended is the use of the Fathers and the later Schoolmen in which the priest is to be well-read. From this he will be able to compile a body of divinity, which will be the storehouse of his sermons, The insights of the Fathers are to be weighed against the priest's own insights, for the Holy Spirit teaches in all ages. Such Fathers of the Church become the priest's own teachers and contemporaries, leading him into a deeper knowledge of the Word. This is the classical Anglican use of antiquity along with Scripture and reason, for what the Fathers teach is Scriptural doctrine.

For Herbert, theology was not confined to mere dialectic argument, rational clarity, and systematic thought. It was much more than this. He was steeped in the ancient tradition of *theologia*; a tradition of wisdom and spirit. A contemplative theology in which heart and mind are united—the thirst of the intellect and the drive of the spirit—a quest that reaches beyond the intellectual into the realm of imagination, intuition and wholeness. Such exploration of a fundamental experience of God, available to anyone, implies that the person who prays is a theologian and that the theologian is a person who prays. It is this vision of theology we find in Herbert and he brings it to life by showing how it lives in his own experience. He understood and appreciated the relationship between theology and the Church; that the *sui generis* experience of the Church is the source and datum of theology. This implies that there is a critical relationship between the issues of a contemporary world and the daily life of the Church. Hence, Herbert's theology is a contemplative theology that seeks to be radically experiential; a symbolic theology in its immediate, metaphorical and disclosive character. As a result his writing functions through image and symbol, rather than through logic and argument; suggesting more than it literally says, as it connotes both the familiar and the unknown—present experience and future possibility. For the priest such a theology would bear fruit in catechesis, in sermon, and in general conversation. Herbert's expectation is that the priest would work hard at this, so that he would find himself able to communicate a living wisdom of God in his ministrations to his people. He is a reminder of the central importance of theology as a practical science in the life of the Church.

The Priest as Pastor

Walton records the visit of one of Bemerton's parishioners to Herbert on a day when he had gone to repair his rectory.

> ... there came a poor old Woman, with an intent to acquaint him with her necessitous condition, as also, with some troubles of her mind; but after she had spoke some few words to him she was surpriz'd with a fear, and that begot a short-ness of breath, so that her spirits and speech fail'd her; which he perceiving did so compassionate her, and was so humble that he took her by the hand, and said, 'Speak good Mother, be not afraid to speak to me; for I am a man that will hear you with patience; and will relieve your necessities too, if I be able: and this I will do willingly, and therefore, Mother, be not afraid to acquaint me with what you desire....'

The outcome was that he helped and comforted her, and discovering that she came from his parish, told her that he would take care of her. As this cost him nothing, he gave her some money and sent her home, 'with a cheerful heart, praising God and praying for him.' Walton comments that thus was Herbert lowly in his own eyes and lovely in the eyes of others. In the mantel of the chimney in the hall of his rectory he had engraved some words for his successor:

> To my Successor.
> If thou chance for to find
> A new House to thy mind,
> And built without thy Cost:
> Be good to the Poor,
> As God gives thee store,
> And then my Labour's not lost.

The pastor is to bring to his people the compassionate heart of God, and this is what characterizes the ministry of Herbert as a pastor. He was diligent in visiting his people and in comforting the sick, in building up relationships with them, and in bringing reconciliation to those at enmity with one another, but above all in praying for them. His effectiveness as a teacher and pastor lies in his own witness, the priest who always practised first what he taught to others.

The Priest Today

The task of a priest may be different in many respects today, and even perhaps more difficult, but the principles upon which Herbert built his life as a priest are of universal application. Perhaps his priesthood can best be summed up by seeing it as a balance between *diakonia* and *doulos*. In his engagement and service to his people, *diakonia*, there was always that deep relationship with God from whom everything emanated and to whom everything was offered. That relationship with God is best described by the word slave or *doulos*, for to be a slave meant to be possessed utterly by another, with no claims, no rights, no earnings, no independent status of one's own. The other who thus possesses a man is God. The priest is Christ's slave; Christ himself took the form of a slave and became obedient to death. So while the priest serves human needs, he lives a Godward life; witnessing that only when lives are utterly possessed by God do they find their true freedom.

This is the priest's message to the world of today; a world that has become dominated by a Post-Renaissance humanism that has occupied the last three centuries. It was the message of Herbert who pre-dated that irruption of thought into western European life and culture, but also that which gave meaning and purpose to the life of the philosopher Bishop Butler, who was sensitive to the initial effects of this in the rising tide of atheism. The defect of this humanism lies in what Maritain describes as an *anthropocentric* concept of man and culture. He uses the term to describe man shut up in himself and separated from

Nature, Grace and God.

> And for human life, for the concrete movement of history, this means real and serious amputations, prayer, evangelical virtues, supra-rational truths, sense of sin and of grace and of the Gospel's beatitudes, the necessity for self-sacrifice and ascetic discipline, for contemplation, for the means of the Cross—all this has either been stuck between parentheses or finally denied.[10]

The promise of the Renaissance was in the conviction that things that had previously been obscure were now being explained and that in the place of 'dogmatic' or 'unscientific' explanations which no longer satisfied the mind, the 'true explanation' of things was now coming to light, hence the reason for it being called the 'enlightenment'.[11] It will be helpful to return to the insights of Newbigin[12] who points out that in 1983 these expectations have not been realized, the heavenly city has not arrived and we do not expect it, nor does the world appear to us more rational than it did in previous centuries. Science may well have traced the necessary relations between things and given them expression in the laws of nature, one of the greatest achievements of the human spirit, but the result has been a world without meaning. His conviction is that our problems will not be solved within the terms provided by our own culture, a culture that has permitted the Church to live as a privileged minority, but has relegated it to a private sphere and faith to a private opinion. A culture whose public life is controlled by a totally different vision of reality. In consequence, Newbigin writes that it would be hard to deny that contemporary western Christianity is in an advanced state of syncretism in its uncritical acceptance of many of the assumptions of contemporary culture. It has thus almost lost the power to address a radical challenge to that vision, and therefore to 'modern western civilization' as a whole. When theological thought becomes *anthropocentric,* it becomes an expression of humanity's egocentricism, rather than of God's revelation. When such a theological tendency resides within

the Church it speaks the language of faith, but changes the
contents and terms in the process. Its centre is no longer in
Christ's Cross, but in man—in his desires and supposed needs.

Newbigin's plea is for a new starting point. One which
while not demeaning the achievements of modern culture,
does not reduce Christian faith and life to the plausibility
structure of modern thought, nor to an optional private
opinion held under the shadow of another world-view.
Following Polanyi, his concern is to shift the balance of faith
and doubt in the whole enterprise of understanding. He
wishes to have recognized the point that doubt—though
always an essential ingredient—is also always secondary,
and that it is faith which is fundamental. Both men see a
clue in St Augustine, in that what happened at the inception
of the Renaissance was the opposite of that effected by
Augustine. The Renaissance turned away from Christian
dogma to the spirit and method of Hellenic man, hence the
resemblance of post-Renaissance secular man to Hellenic
man. Essentially this found expression in the belief in the
autonomy of human reason and conscience and in the right
of every person to the maximum possible happiness. It also
found expression in the nation-state as the entity to which
one looks for the securing of rights, and in the methods of
modern science as the means for understanding and control-
ling events. In Augustine's day Hellenic culture had ceased
to be a meaningful framework for living. Augustine provided
the new framework, which began with the Incarnation and
claimed the acceptance by faith of this revelation. This
provided the starting point for the endless enterprise of
understanding, articulated in the doctrine of the Trinity. The
sine qua non for this new understanding was *faith*, not as the
destination, but as the beginning from which understanding
emerges. Some few hundred years later Anselm reiterated
this '*credo ut intelligam*: I believe in order that I might
understand.'

The parallels between our own situation and Augustine's
are obvious and we can only give due credit to the brilliance
of achievement. Yet if the achievements of autonomous

reason have produced a sense of meaninglessness and hopelessness, then we may find light and hope in the suggested agreement of Polanyi and Newbigin, that we need to look for renewal beyond 'the framework of the assumptions which the Enlightenment held to be self-evident, that there is needed a radical conversion, a new starting point which begins as an act of trust in divine grace as something simply given to be received in faith and gratitude.'[13] Augustine who is only reiterating that whole patristic orientation which converted Hellenic man, is not seen as a model but by way of analogy. Following Polanyi's plea for a 'post-critical philosophy' as the pre-condition for the renewal of our culture, and staking our future on consciously a-critical statements, Newbigin warns that this can only be done within the full acknowledgement of the irreversible nature of the last 250 years. He quotes Polanyi who claims that he is seeking to establish and:

> ... to restore to us once more the power for the deliberate holding of unproven beliefs. We should be able to profess now, knowingly and openly, those beliefs which could be tacitly taken for granted in the days before modern philosophic criticism reached its present incisiveness. Such powers may appear dangerous. But a dogmatic orthodoxy can be kept in check both internally and eternally, while a creed inverted into a science is both blind and deceptive.[14]

While the Church has always claimed that the Gospel on offer cannot be demonstrated, but must be accepted in faith. Polanyi's proposal is that:

> 'Not just in the private sector but also in the public world another model for understanding is needed; that this in turn requires the acknowledgement that our most fundamental beliefs cannot be demonstrated but are held by faith; that it is the responsibility of the Church to offer this new model for understanding as the basis for a radical renewal of our culture; and that without such radical renewal our culture has no future. This is—if one may put it very sharply—an invitation to recover a proper acknowledgement of the role of dogma. It

is an invitation to the Church to be bold in offering to the men and women of our culture a way of understanding which makes no claim to be demonstrable in the terms of 'modern' thought, which is not 'scientific' in the popular use of that word, which is based unashamedly on the revelation of God made man in Jesus Christ and attested in scripture and the tradition of the Church, and which is offered as a fresh starting point for the exploration of the mystery of human existence and for coping with its practical tasks, not only in the private and domestic life of the believers, but also in the public life of the citizen.[15]

The task of the priest will be to clarify something of the tradition that lives in him; the tradition in which Herbert and Butler lived and in which he lives; the tradition of wisdom and spirit that is found in Anglicanism, but also more widely in Western Christendom, and which has its roots in Scripture and the Fathers. His task will be to keep alive a continuous sense of what has been valid in the past, bringing this to life by showing how it continues to live in his own experience, and thereby giving it contemporary relevance by supplanting the *anthropocentric* stance of man and culture, with a way of *theocentric* living. It will be an existential disposing of himself in the way of Christ. The expression of a practical or ecclesial Christology, in which the focus of this living of the mystery of Christ in which his life is rooted, will be the *Liturgy, prayer* and *spirituality.* Here in the realm of dogma as salvation, in the *sui generis* experience of the Church as *New Life*, he will find the wellsprings of renewal for himself, for the Church and contemporary culture. The new and sharp perspective he brings will not be a piece of mere thinking, but the lived experience of the mysteries of Christ. The Life which is salvation, which is given *now* in present experience for the renewal and transformation of creation and life. The Church is its continuity and fulfilment in this world, and is therefore, something concrete and living, which is deeply rooted in the ordinary lives of people, and in the everyday life of that pastoral context in which the priest carries out his ministry. Here priest and people together come into a living relationship with events and realities that cannot be trapped within the contours of thought or language. For these events and realities are not to be apprehended, yet through them— and by way of stillness, attention, openness, love and communion—we glimpse the invisible just as God appre- hends us. This is the way of *credo ut intelligam,* the way of Augustine and Anselm. A life mystical and sacramental that reaches beyond the merely intellectual into the realm of imagination, intuition or wholeness.

This is not a retreat into *antiquarianism* or *primitivism,* for it is not merely a return to the past. Nor is it a search for some 'golden age' that will act as a period of reference *par excellence.* What Lossky says of Lancelot Andrewes can equally apply to the priest of today.

> The 'tradition' of the Church is not the simple conservation of what has been said and done in the past. It is a dynamic process that transcends linear time, without in any way abolishing it. It is in fact a way of living in time in the light of eternity, which recapitulates past, present, and future because everything is lived in contemporaneity with the reality of the Gospel. 'What the churches of God have done at all times' is [important] not in the spirit of imitation or conservatism, but to the extent that they have done it in a consciousness of living by *memorial, anamnesis*, the past events of the Gospel and their consequences to come, in the Church of the present.[16]

The result will not be a theology lacking in originality, unless one means by theology merely the elaboration of a coherent system of thought about God.

> But if... to make a theology means to make more and more truly one's own, by experience, the mystery of the relation of God to man that has been traditionally lived by the Church, then originality will consist not so much in innovation, as in enabling the whole era to grasp the genuine essence of the Christian message. In fact, the more a theologian penetrates into the heart of the mystery, the more his teaching will be personal, and consequently original.[17]

The journey into such an experience of theological awareness is by way of liturgy, prayer and spirituality, that will enable us to speak in such a way to our contemporaries that our message will continue to live beyond our time.

Notes

1. Walton, *Lives* (Falcon Educational Books, 1951), p. 227.
2. Walton, *ibid.*, p. 216.
3. Walton, *ibid.*, p. 228.
4. Sidney Lee (ed.), *Lord Cherbury, An Autobiography* (1906), p. 11, cited in *Five Pastorals,* ed. Thomas Wood (SPCK 1961), p. 84.
5. Herbert, *The Country Parson* ch. 1, ed. Thomas Wood, *ibid.,* p. 95.
6. Walton, *ibid.*, p. 242.
7. Herbert, *The Country Parson*, ch. 1, *ibid.* p. 95.
8. Herbert *The Country Parson*, ch. 4, *ibid.,* p. 98.
9. Walton, *ibid.*, p. 230.
10. Jacques Maritain, *The Twilight of Civilization* (Sheed and Ward 1956), p. 10.
11. Newbigin, citing Basil Willey, *European Thought 1680–1720, ibid.*, p. 8.
12. Newbigin, *ibid.*, p. 17.
13. Newbigin, *ibid.*, p. 25.
14. Polanyi, *Personal Knowledge* (1958), p. 268.
15. Newbigin, *ibid.*, p. 27.
16. N. Lossky, *Lancelot Andrewes the Preacher*, trans. A. Louth (Clarendon Press, Oxford 1991), p. 340.
17. N. Lossky, *ibid.*, p. 6.

3

Our Theological Teacher

For a priest to incorporate the way of Christ into his whole being will require that he centre his life within the total and living experience of the Church, which constitutes the source and datum of theology. Here the issue of theology is discovered to be, in the phrase of Michael Ramsey, 'not only one of intellectual clarity, but of a union of human lives with God in the way of holiness'. Theology is both existential and mystical, the description of an experience rather than a definition. It can only be fully understood by conforming one's life to doctrine. As the great nineteenth-century ex-Unitarian Anglican theologian F.D. Maurice, wrote:

> The Liturgy has been to me a great theological teacher; a perpetual testimony that the Father, the Son and the Spirit, the one God blessed for ever, is the author of all life, freedom, unity to men; that our prayers are nothing but responses to His voice speaking to us and in us.

What Maurice meant by that can be seen by looking at the *Alternative Service Book* or the *Book of Common Prayer*. These must not merely be considered as manuals of public devotions. In them, more so in the *BCP*, you will find the fullest statement of the teaching of the Church. In its lections from Holy Scripture, its creeds, prayers, thanksgivings, exhortations, confessions, absolutions and occasional offices, it brings before us all the great articles of the Christian Faith in what we may call their natural order and proportion. It places them in their organic relation to other truths, and gives constant practical reference to their subjective aspects. *The Articles* and *Formularies of our Church* set forth these doctrines as objective truths; the *ASB* and *BCP* connect them directly with our spiritual needs and our daily conduct.

In the quotation given above, Maurice is actually saying that the *sui generis* experience of the Church is the source and reference point of theology. There is an ecclesial context to Anglican divinity which understands the Church as bearing witness to the truth, not merely by reminiscence or from the words of others, but from its own living, unceasing experience, and out of its Catholic fullness which has its roots in continuity with the Primitive Church. Therein consists the 'tradition of truth' in which the apostolic teaching is not so much an unchangeable example to be repeated or imitated, as an eternally living and inexhaustible source of life and inspiration. Is not this what the Orthodox call 'Holy Tradition'? A life both mystical and sacramental. A constant abiding Spirit rather than the mere memory of words. A charismatic, not an historical principle, and one which when taken together with Scripture contains the truth of divine revelation. A truth that lives in the Church.

This ecclesial character of Christian theologising has been one of the outstanding characteristics of the English Church in all the principal periods of its life, and is also what distinguished it from Protestantism as it developed on the Continent. As a result of its effect the English Church was saved from what befell so many Protestant bodies on the Continent, and avoided being saddled with a dominant theological idea of a kind that might prove a mental and spiritual incubus to later generations. To quote George Florovsky:

> Apart from life in Christ theology carries no conviction, and, if separated from the life of faith, theology may easily degenerate into empty dialectics, a vain *polylogia*, without any spiritual consequence. Patristic theology was rooted in the decisive commitment of faith. It was not just a self-explanatory 'discipline' which could be presented argumentatively, *i.e. Aristotelikos*, without a prior spiritual engagement. This theology

could only be 'preached' or 'proclaimed' and not be
simply 'taught' in a school manner; 'preached' from
the pulpit, proclaimed also in the word of prayer and
sacred rites and indeed manifested in the total structure
of Christian life. Theology of this kind can never be
separated from the life of prayer and from the practice
of virtue. 'The climax of purity is the beginning of
theology'[1], in the phrase of St John Klimakos.[2]

It is only the pure in heart who see God. Purity must precede
vision, as vision must precede theology.

An Eschatological Experience[3]

To speak of the priest as a man of liturgy is to speak of his
immersion in an experience which has profound implications
for his life as a man of prayer, theology and pastoral
concern. His immersion is not primarily in an idea or a
doctrine, but as stated, in an experience in which with his
people he finds himself living. This experience is not in
terms of individual religious experience, but is an immersion
in the *sui generis* experience of the Church; the Church as
experience of new reality, new experience, new life. Such
experience is not in terms of some 'other world', but rather
of this world, creation and life, renewed and transformed in
Christ, transposed into the knowledge of and communion
with God and his Kingdom. This is what constitutes life in
Christ and is to be 'hidden with Christ in God', implying
that the Church by her very nature belongs to the reality of
the world to come. Our knowledge and constant partaking of
the *eschaton*, the *end*, is what relates us as the Church to the
world, providing us with the only source of the 'victory that
overcomes the world'. This world can never set the agenda
for the Church, because it is only in and through this
ecclesial experience of the Kingdom of God that the world
becomes the object of our love, providing our agenda for the
world in all its saving and transforming power. Only in this
experience of the Church, the subject and source of our data,
can we as men of theology know God, and in God, Man,

Society, Nature, and Life.

As a man of liturgy the priest immerses himself in this eschatological experience. This entails opening himself to a present experience of the Kingdom. For too long such eschatological experience has been relegated to a static doctrine of the four last things, to be preached in Advent or to occupy the last four chapters of a theological text-book. Essential for today's Church is a recovery of the primitive and much more dynamic understanding of eschatology as a dimension of present experience. To recover it in this way is to make it a partner in life and ministry, allowing it to shape and permeate the whole of Christian Faith and life. For the man of theology it becomes a way of looking at and experiencing the world; but with the kingdom of God and not the world as the ultimate term of reference.

This eschatological dimension of experience has already been given to us in Christ, not as something yet to come, but as something which has already come and will come in all its fullness at the end of time. The Kingdom has come in Jesus Christ, Incarnate, crucified, risen, ascended, and in the fruit of Pentecost. Therefore it is already present in the Church, the *ecclesia* of those who have been baptized into Christ's death and Resurrection, and who live in newness of life eating and drinking in his Kingdom, and so partaking of His Spirit.

The Liturgy

This eschatological experience of faith is primarily given and received in the Church's rule of prayer and worship. The liturgy becomes the epiphany and manifestation of new life, as the Eucharist becomes the sacrament of Christ's coming and presence. In its essential meaning it is eschatological and ecclesiological, and thereby central and unique to the Church's life. Here on the Lord's Day, the first day of the new creation, rooted in the resurrection of Christ, Christ, the Life and Light of men, comes into the midst of his own at

the weekly Easter. The First Day is also the Eighth, because
to partake of the life of God is to participate in that which
is beyond time. So the Eighth day becomes the figure of life
everlasting, the symbol of eternity in which we now live
because of Christ. Therefore it is the day without evening,
the last day, because no other day can follow eternity. Hence
the Eucharist always makes the Church what she is, the
Body of Christ and the Temple of the Holy Spirit.

As the Liturgy is to be central to the Church's life so it
becomes central for the priest's life and ministry, making the
faith of the Church its very source and datum. Such eschatological experience gives wholeness to his thinking and
praying as it brings his mind and spirit into a living relationship with certain events, making him a constant witness and
participant in these events, their saving, life-giving and
transfiguring reality. What is disclosed is that the Church's
faith cannot be divorced from her experience of these events,
nor can they be known in their rational meaning outside the
experience that reveals their reality. For it brings one into
direct encounter with living, saving and transforming Truth,
beyond the limitations of a given 'situation' or 'Age' or
culture. At the same time, in the spirit of the pastor he will
lead his people away from philosophies and ideas that can
only bring spiritual death, by bringing them into this same
direct and life-giving knowledge of the Truth in which they
will be saved and transformed.

This is not a reduction of theology to liturgy. It is rather
the way in which we can allow the eschatological experience
of the liturgy to enlarge our vision of the theological task,
and at the same time to deliver us from a too restrictive
understanding of liturgy. Too often in this age of individualism it has been narrowly interpreted in subjective terms as
the mere inspiration and sanctification of the individual, a
procedure through which I receive 'my Communion'. Yet in
being central and unique to the Church's life it is the
epiphany in which is manifested the Church's faith, making
the Church what she is, witness and participant of the saving
event of Christ, of the presence in the world of the *New Life*

of the Kingdom to come. Baptism by water and the Spirit into the death and resurrection of the Lord, makes it possible for us to assemble as the ecclesia on the First and Eighth Day to hear his Word as we eat and drink at his table in his Kingdom. This is no cultic ritualism, but the immersion of the whole *ecclesia* in the liturgy of time, as she brings the whole universe and all eternity to Christ to 'fill all things with himself', and in this way fulfils her very nature in response to her cosmological and eschatological vocation. Through the Liturgy the Lord of the Church keeps the *ecclesia* informed of that vocation, giving her the power to fulfil it and become what she truly is: the sacrament of the new creation; the sacrament in Christ of the Kingdom.

In the best sense of the word, the *ecclesia* is a realm of grace, a communion of persons living in the life that Christ shares with the Father in the Holy Spirit; the *New Life* and knowledge of God in his Kingdom. The *lex credendi*, the rule of faith, is something given and experienced in the *lex orandi*, the rule of prayer and worship. Being organically related to one another they cannot be separated without damage to both, so that the Liturgy is the *loci theologici*. Here in the realm of faith as experience, our theology will recover its wholeness in the catholic vision and experience of God, Christ, Man, and the Church-in-the-world. Being a man of liturgy has a theological consequence for the priest, in that we become theologians in a complete sense. Men who can see the true fecundity of theological and spiritual problems, because of the fullness of insight which God himself initiates. In various parishes in which I have worked, I have introduced parishioners to a liturgical celebration of Holy Week, bringing together theology and liturgy in an experience of the saving events of the *Paschal Mystery*. Their response has never ceased to amaze me. They have been the first to admit that never before have they so clearly understood the mysteries of creation, death and resurrection. Their understanding of the *mysterion* has come, not by a rational digest of ancient texts, but by a lived experience of the very saving events in and through the liturgy. Every year it becomes for them a time of renewal as they enter ever more deeply into this experience of faith, and find their minds enlightened through the experience and thoughts of their hearts.

Anglican Precedent

There is precedent in Anglicanism for the spirit and principle of what is written here. The keeping together of theology and experience; intellect and intuition; thinking and praying. Commenting upon the tragedy of these things becoming separated from each other in the contemporary world, Canon Allchin emphasises that Anglicanism has always sought to keep them together. He cites such figures as Jeremy Taylor, Joseph Butler, F.J.A. Hort, F.D. Maurice and William Temple, and one could list many others. These men strove for an ideal of theology which was not divorced from prayer and liturgy; for a way of life and worship which is informed and structured by theological vision. He goes on:

> The growth of the person in grace is something different from simple individualism. It is as we are being freed from our individual restrictions that we begin to taste the liberty of persons, the freedom of the sons of God. This involves a religion which is neither that of heart and mind, of feeling or intellect, but which is characterised by the mad fervour of the great theologians and spiritual writers of East and West alike, who have discovered the secret of 'putting the mind in the heart'.[4]

In viewing the priest as a man of liturgy, we glimpse a vision of liturgy that is more than a collection of services, and the priest as more than the professionally religious person whose job it is in the popular mind to take services. The emphasis is on an understanding of the inner meaning of liturgy and its underlying principles, and a sense that liturgy has something to do with dogma and life. The priest's participation in it is the starting point of his prayer life, the environment in which his own personal prayer will live and grow. Only in so far as he grasps in a living way the interior connections between dogma, prayer and life, will he be able to assist his people to grasp hold of such realities. Addlestraw writes:

> The Church, if it is to win the fight against modern paganism, and not only win the fight but heal the wounds inflicted by this paganism on man's nature, needs to re-integrate a new wholeness, in which the dogma, the prayer and the life form a living unity.[5]

Addleshaw goes on to see a relevance for today's liturgical renewal in seventeenth-century Anglican liturgical thinking as it can be found in Hooker, Andrewes, Thorndike, Cosin and others of that school. These men did not view liturgy in isolation as a collection of services, but emphasised an understanding of its inner meaning and underlying principles. For them liturgy was not divorced from dogma and life. Their purpose was restoration, not the producing of something new nor the emasculating of Christian truth by trying to reconcile it with the spirit of the age. They were for the most part parish priests, dealing with ordinary people and their difficulties, and their teaching was couched in a language, and presented in a way that ordinary people could understand. For them the Church is an organism, and dogma, prayer and life are one whole. Their contribution to Anglican liturgical thought was in their lives as much as in their writings. How they prayed the liturgy was as important as how they ordered it, so that people caught from them the spirit of liturgical prayer.

Their Sources of Inspiration

Within the scope of this book it is not possible to consider these men in any detail, but some consideration of the general background of their sources of inspiration will be helpful. Anglican parochial life had broken down so that the majority were ignorant of the meaning of the *Prayer Book* and badly in need of instruction in the principles of liturgical worship. Exposition, and defence of the principles of liturgy was necessary all through the seventeenth century, which like the twentieth century was characterized by individualism. However these men gave due place to liturgy in the life of the Church and grasped its implications. The source of their inspiration was beyond the parochialism of their nation, age or culture, in *the appeal to antiquity*, enabling them to transcend the limitations of nationalism and what was merely cultural. They set out to restore the grandeur of Christian truth, and to teach it anew to their countrymen who had largely forgotten it in the turmoil of the Reformation.

Addleshaw continues:

> It is a theology characterized by a veneration for the Fathers, by wholeness finding its centre in the Incarnation and a massive learning. Instead of trying to create a scientific system of theology on the plan of Suarez or Calvin, they take seriously the claim of the English Reformers to be returning to antiquity. They turned to the Fathers and there, in Dean Church's words found something 'to enrich, to enlarge, to invigorate, to give beauty, proportion, and force to their theology'. The patristic basis makes their theology something *sui generis*, something quite different from Tridentinism or continental Protestantism.[6]

All the time they work in terms of patristic thought, more especially the Greek Fathers, so that the vision one finds in them has about it the catholicity, wide-mindedness, the freshness, the suppleness, and sanity of Christian antiquity. Here they learned to see the Christian Faith as an integral whole, quite naturally finding its centre in the Incarnation. A look at Andrewes' sermons will demonstrate how he deals with the central facts of the Creed in relation to one another and as forming a whole, nowhere stressing one aspect of Christian truth with the consequent impoverishment of the whole faith. As Dean Church comments, with their theology centred in the Incarnation, it ends in adoration, self-surrender, and blessing, and in the awe and joy of welcoming the presence of the Eternal Beauty, the Eternal Sanctity, and the Eternal Love, the Sacrifice and Reconciliation of the world. They were men of liturgy, spirituality, and prayer, in which they found the seeds of their theology, and because they were parish priests it is couched in a language and presented in a way which the ordinary layman of their day could understand, as they made their theology something of concern and interest to the whole Church and expounded it in sermons to ordinary congregations. It was never learning for learning's sake, but learning acquired with devotion and self-sacrifice, that they might lead their countrymen from the spiritual desert in which they had been left at the Reformation, to the pastures of eternal truth.

> Their standard of reference is always the first four or five centuries, which they looked on as a liturgical golden age. Their desire to bring their countrymen to the eternal truth is reflected in their desire that the liturgy should be something in which all can share, that it should be grounded on dogma. The importance they attached to the Incarnation tended to make them find the centre of the Liturgy in the Cross; it led them to see that the liturgy must itself witness to the truth that the totality of man's nature, both as an individual and a social being, is capable of being redeemed and offered to God. The Fathers taught them to think of the Church as an organism, and to see that dogma, prayer and life are one whole.[7]

Reading the Fathers

It was this patristic dimension in their theology which gave to these divines that principle of integration that enabled them to maintain the organic connections between dogma, prayer and life. This principle is essential to the life of any divine, not least, those of us in the parishes. In the nineteenth century, J.J. Blunt, the Lady Margaret Professor at Cambridge, was concerned to revive the study of the Fathers among those preparing for the priesthood; and the evangelical Bishop Kaye of Lincoln had made this his priority when Regius Professor at Cambridge in that same period. Among

Blunt's lectures there is a series on the duties of the parish priest. Three of these lectures are directed to the *Reading of the Parish Priest*.[8] His concern was not to recommend a catalogue of books, a multiplication of authors which only create a confusion of knowledge in young divines. His object was rather to suggest a method of reading; certain principles by which clergy could govern their study. He advises the reading of Anglican divines, as auxiliaries rather than as principals, and aims to suggest a few master-keys, thereby rendering the acquisition of a few special keys less needful, and so deliver them from those ruts of theology in modern names and schools. In encouraging the reading of the Fathers, Blunt argues that here the young divine will encounter an original authority and along with the study of the original Scriptures, 'will have possessed yourselves of the very quarry from which all subsequent divines of any note have derived the best materials for their arguments (whatever might be the subject of them)'.[9] Not only will it lead the reader to his own originality of thought, it will also equip him to derive more benefit from Anglican theologians or others and impart to him a deeper appreciation of the *Book of Common Prayer* which is a 'compendium of early tradition'.

He lists a number of advantages which follow from such study of the Patriarchs. These briefly amount to the following: such patristic knowledge will inform the reader of the genuine text and Canon of Scripture and enable one to see how many of the old heresies have persisted in a different key; from such first-hand knowledge, one is equipped to defend true doctrine from false, using the patristic arguments and affirming the unanimous opinion of the Primitive Church; the doctrine of the Church of England is grounded in the Holy Scriptures, and in such teachings of the ancient Fathers and Councils as are agreeable to the same. In recourse to such authorities one will find the source and justification for the ethos and polity of Anglicanism. One could add that the whole spectrum of liturgy with which we are concerned—not only the *Book of Common Prayer* but

the entire movement for liturgical renewal in our own time—
is patristic in ethos and orientation because it is a return to
these sources.

Liturgical Prayer and Liturgical Spirituality[10]

The priest as a man of liturgy will become also a man of
theology. In him dogma, prayer and life shall find an
integration, if only the liturgy is allowed to become, in the
spirit of Maurice, 'a great theological teacher, a perpetual
testimony that the Father, the Son and the Spirit the one God
blessed for ever, is the author of all life, freedom, unity to
men; that our prayers are nothing but responses to his voice
speaking to us and in us'. He will also need to be a man of
faith in the sense that Abraham was a man of faith. A man
whose life was lived on God's terms, and whose perseverance in faith led to the fulfilment of God's promises. This is
the Augustinian starting point for the way of understanding
mentioned in the previous chapter; a faith leading to a
relationship of grateful acceptance of what God has in store
for us, and in which priority and pride of place is given to
trusting in God's promises. In such dependence on God
everything is seen as a grace from God, to which the priest
responds with humble acceptance, grateful praise, and
thanks; the attitudes of Christian worship.

It is God who always takes the initiative. It is he who
gives the invitation to a relationship in faith and love as in
faith we respond and offer prayer, worship and our lives in
service, relying on his fidelity as we gather for the prayer we
call 'liturgy'. Such faith on our part is necessary for liturgy
and sacraments to make sense, but that faith is fed and
grows, as the promises made in baptism are made again and
again in our hearts at the Church's experience of common
faith profession, the liturgy. The use of the word spirituality
describes the experience of our relationship with God in faith
and the ways in which we live it out. Spirituality involves
our coming to know God and our response to God in the

prayer and work we perform in faith; a response that occurs in and among the Christian community, whose members are themselves formed by hearing and responding to the same call and invitation from God.

As a man of spirituality the priest's prayer is community-centred. It involves the ready response to the word of God in prayer and action with others and alone. His spirituality can never be self-contained, self-serving or self-concerned. It must aim to integrate the many facets of his life and ministry in communion with others and in relationship with God. His experience of prayer will shape how he views the world, how he acts in the world, and how he witnesses to the enduring power of the word of God in the world. A spirituality derived from the liturgy does not mean the abandoning of personal prayer, for it is these moments of prayer that enliven his response to God's call and deepen his faith. What the liturgy will contribute to his spirituality is a mode of prayer shared by the whole Church; it will therefore provide an important basis and foundation for his spiritual life. In Office and Eucharist, his life and ministry are touched, affected, and formed by the Church's spirituality, just as his prayer and spirituality are derived from it.

There is, however, a distinction between liturgical prayer, that is the experience of the liturgy, and liturgical spirituality. Liturgical prayer involves readings and proclamations; prayers and symbolic actions in which the Christian community respond to the work of Christ. Here priest and people take bread, water and wine and place them in a liturgical experience that they may be transformed by the words of prayer so that the *ecclesia* may share again and again in that new life which is salvation. From this experience of liturgical prayer, liturgical spirituality (which is much wider) is given focus and direction. Because of this it can give us a way of looking at all creation—the events of our own lives, and of all humanity through the perspective of the *Paschal Mystery*, that is central to Christian worship. Christ has died, Christ has risen, Christ will come again. This fundamentally Incarnational view is extended beyond our liturgical functions as priests, and comes to shape how we pray, reflect, and act outside the experience of liturgy.

How we look at life will be affected by our participation in the liturgy. In the Eucharist, in the Office and in the reflections it feeds us as we move through the Christian year. The dogmatic basis that underlies this passage of time brings before us Creation, Incarnation, Atonement, Resurrection, the Work of the Spirit and Transfiguration. Christmas and the Incarnation remind us of the presence of God, the Logos at work in all creation, as well as of the possibilities for the divinization and thereby transfiguration of all humanity graced by this mystery of Christ. Not only does it bring us into a new relationship with each other, it brings us into a new relation with all creation; the new creation which now exists in Christ. To speak of the priest as a man of liturgy, spirituality and prayer implies more than an engagement in liturgical rites, as he focuses on that which has a formative influence in the development, not only of his own spirituality, but on the spirituality of the Christian community as a whole.

Liturgical Prayer and Personal Prayer

Participation in liturgical prayer fosters ways of acting in response to prayer and influences the way one prays outside the liturgy. When one looks at the Christian Mystical Tradition one sees that there is no dichotomy or conflict between liturgy and personal prayer, for they are two aspects of the Christian's praying which are essentially mutually inclusive. Thomas Merton[11] sees this conflict between 'public' and 'private' prayer as a modern 'pseudo-problem'. As he writes, 'Liturgy by its very nature tends to prolong itself in individual contemplative prayer, and mental prayer in its turn disposes us for and seeks fulfilment in liturgical worship.' We may well ponder Michael Ramsey's words on this matter written in the 1960s in his book *Sacred and Secular*.

> Liturgical movements strive to bridge the gap between worship and the common life, and just now they gather to

themselves much enthusiasm and romance. But will these movements succeed unless there is with them a revival of contemplative prayer? There are signs, not perhaps many, but enough to be significant, of a new discovery of contemplative prayer in the setting of everyday life. Contemplative prayer is the hunger and thirst, of desire for God.... Such is the prayer that links Christianity and ordinary life.[12]

Liturgical and spiritual renewal are inter-related and there can be no emergence of effective worship until both kinds of renewal are taken to heart.

Nathan Mitchell pinpoints this inter-relationship where he writes:

> Personal prayer explodes into the speech of public praise and sacramental action, while the speech of worship erupts into the still point' of silence where, as T.S. Eliot says, 'there is only the dance'. The prayer of the heart structures the experience of worship, while worship shapes the content of personal prayer.[13]

This implies the need to penetrate beneath the outward trappings to the essence of liturgy, that we might comprehend its inner meaning and implications as we give liturgical worship a place in the life of the soul. Such an understanding and appreciation of the experience of liturgy will increase our awareness of what kind of personal prayer can be derived from it and how one's conduct and life choices should be shaped by it. A delicate balance is required between liturgy as a unique experience of God in common prayer and as a means for ordering one's spirituality, and the need to avoid at all costs the reduction of liturgical texts to ideology or programmes of action. The counter-productive face of liturgical renewal is the expert in instant and fluid liturgy, the concocting of attractive forms of service for the imparting of information (usually of a political or social nature), the striving to make people feel good, and to experience something pleasurable and immediately understandable. As Colin Dunlop points out:

Whenever worship is thought of as essentially a means to some other human end, however lofty, its pursuit will surely be disappointing. Such an estimate is bound up with an ultimate belief that God exists for man and heaven for earth, and that nothing is of value unless it can be shown to contribute a more or less immediate benefit to man assessable in terms of this world.[14]

Liturgy is not an ideology, nor is it a self-contained cultic action. To reduce it to such is to put it out of focus. It is ecclesiological in character not cultic, and exists in and for the Church. To allow it to exist and be celebrated in and for itself cannot lead to a spirituality described as 'liturgical'. An appropriate response is required by and derived from the celebration of the liturgy, and the whole aim of liturgical renewal has been to reunite liturgy with the devotional life of all Christians. In discovering this harmony between his experience of liturgical prayer and the rest of his spirituality—what is best described as a level of integration—the priest will be enabled to lead his people into such an integrated spirituality.

Personal prayer will naturally and rightly be affected by one's experience of liturgical prayer, as one unselfconsciously uses its language. With the intention and language of liturgical prayer woven into one's personal prayer, one begins to pray in the spirit of the whole Body, which gathers into itself the experience of the saints, contemporary fellow-members, martyrs and confessors of previous ages. Hence our personal prayer is caught up in the rich and diverse experience of the prayer of God's people through the ages. This enlarges the parochialism of our own personal experience, bringing a vision of the height, depth, and width of relationship God allows us to share with him. The Liturgy becomes a school where we catch something of the essence of prayer, and see our personal prayer as nothing private, but as a part of the prayer the whole creation addresses to its Creator. There will be no antipathy as each finds an essential integration and interdependence.

Notes

1.   St John Klimakos, *Scala Paradisi*, Grade 30.
2.   G. Florovsky, *Aspects of Church History* (Nordland 1975), p. 17.
3.   A. Schmemann, *Church, World and Mission* (SVP 1979). I am indebted to some insights on eschatology and liturgy which I have developed in my own way.
4.   A.M. Allchin, *Christian*, Autumn 1976 (All Saints Margaret Street Institute of Christian Studies).
5.   G.W.O. Addleshaw, *The High Church Tradition, A Study in the Liturgical Thought of the 17th Century* (Faber 1941), p. 17.
6.   Addleshaw, *ibid.*, p. 25.
7.   Addlleshaw, *ibid.*, p. 30.
8.   *Blunt's Parish Priest* ch. 3 (1856), Lecture 3.
9.   *Ibid.*
10.   Kevin Irwin, *Liturgy, Prayer and Spirituality* (Paulist Press, New York / Ramsey, 1984). Chapter 1 has a useful discussion of this theme and has provided some valuable insights.
11.   Thomas Merton, *Contemplative Prayer* (DLT 1973), p. 55.
12.   Michael Ramsey, *Sacred and Secular,* (Longmans 1967), p. 57.
13.   Nathan Mitchell, *Christians at Prayer* (University of Notre Dame Press, 1977), p. 19, cited by Irwin, *ibid.*, p. 18.
14.   C. Dunlop, *Anglican Public Worship* (SCM 1961), p. 10.

4

The Daily Office

Bells

The Book of Common Prayer requires that every deacon and priest shall say daily and publicly Mattins and Evensong, unless 'let by sickness', when he is to say it with his family. Before saying *The Daily Office* he must first 'cause' the bell to be tolled, an action more significant than we realize, for it is the carrier of a message to the community at large. Thomas Merton tells us that bells are the voice of our alliance with the God of heaven, reminding us that we are his true temple and calling us to peace with Him within ourselves.

> The bells say: 'We have spoken for centuries from the towers of great Churches. We have spoken to the saints your fathers, in their land. We called them, as we call you to sanctity. What is the word with which we called them?
>
> 'We did not merely say, "Be good, come to Church." We did not merely say "Keep the commandments" but above all, "Christ is risen, Christ is risen!" And we said: "Come with us, God is good, salvation is not hard, His love has made it easy!" And this our message, has always been for everyone, for those who came and for those who did not come, for our song is perfect as the Father in heaven is perfect and we pour our charity out upon all.'[1]

Writing of the sacramental quality of church buildings, Solzhenitsyn, in a Russia where the human Christian voice was muted, writes of hearing the stones cry out proclaiming the Word in Christ.

People were always selfish and often unkind. But the evening chimes used to ring out, floating over villages, field and woods. Reminding men that they must abandon the trivial concerns of this world and give time and thought to eternity.... Our forefathers put all that was finest in themselves, all their understanding of life into these stones, into these bell-towers.[2]

Three years ago at a conference, a woman asked me whether I rang the bell before worship. I replied that I always do, not only before the Eucharist, but also before the Offices. She had convinced her vicar that ringing the bells was worthwhile and rang it for him every day. She invited me to join with her in the prayer she uses as she rings, 'Lord renew me, renew your Church'. I myself now say these words, as well as the prayer of the Angelus in celebration of the Incarnation. An old man once stopped me in the village to tell me that he heard the Angelus ring every day as he sat in the park. If during the hour of six and seven all the bells of every parish church were rung before Evensong every day, what a message we would be ringing to the nation. It is a message I have often heard as I have been walking through the crowded streets of London.

So much for the significance and importance of 'causing the bell to be tolled'. In turning to the *Daily Office*, a book well worth serious study is *Company of Voices* by Fr George Guiver of the Community of the Resurrection. Fr Guiver sub-titles the book *Daily Prayer and the People of God*. His concern, outlined in the Introduction, is that many Christians do not pray. He questions why there should be such a problem, and what can be done about it. His concern is not only with the question 'Why?', in relation to liturgical prayer and *Daily Office*, but in looking at the history of the practice and content; his purpose is to learn from the past for the needs of today.

Within the limits of this book, our concern must be with picking up some of the things he says about content, but at the same time we need to see the pastoral orientation of this essential ingredient of the priest's life of prayer. For those of us who are always alone in the saying of the *Daily Office*, it may be difficult to make real our awareness of this being the corporate action of the People of God, offered in the office and person of ourselves as the priest. One of the saddest trends in recent years has been the decline in Sunday Evensong, encouraged in some places by the clergy themselves because the numbers were small. Ironically the same clergy who had discontinued Evensong when people were coming albeit in small numbers were often the first to complain when no-one at all joined them for Evensong during the week. The faithful remnant at Sunday Evensong may well be the ones who safeguard its continuance into the future, and the springboard from which to develop something during the week. So let us keep it going at all costs.

> One of the chief means provided by God for this gradual conversion of life, which corresponds exactly with our baptism, is the liturgy of the Church: not just the Eucharistic Liturgy, but also the Divine Office. This latter serves to extend the Liturgy of the Word in the Eucharist throughout the day, and makes it broader and fuller and more readily assimilated by those who take part in it. This extended Liturgy of the Word, which we call the Divine Office, provides us, in its own proper mode, with a constantly unfolding revelation of the Mystery of Christ. To help us to appropriate Christ more readily, the structure of the Office leads us into meditation and self-knowledge which is given expression in repentance, praise, and intercession.[3]

In affirming *Light*, as one of the major themes of the Divine Office, Fr Gregory describes it as illuminating both the senses and the intellect and from the moment of our baptism God calls us to open our whole selves to it, for in the resurrection our destiny is to see, know, and love beyond the ordinary capacities of our powers in this lifetime.

> The Divine Office provides a gateway through which the baptized Christian can enter into the new world of the light and freedom of the sons of God; and it has its goal in the Eucharist. We, on our side, may be in need of a renewed faith and expectation that, when we gather together in the name of Jesus Christ and begin our celebration, 'the former things have

passed away' and the new age of the Kingdom has really
come upon us. Without such a renewal in the theological
virtues of faith, hope, and love, any attempts we might make
to revise our worship would hardly amount to more than
academic or aesthetic exercises.[4]

Communal Prayer

The Office is not first and foremost for people's edification.
It is primarily an offering to God—a giving rather than a
getting—and in the spirit of David we come saying 'I will
not offer to the Lord my God that which costs me nothing.'
The name *Office*, emphasizes the conception of the Church's
prayer as her duty, her *officium* to God. So the words used
are not of individual devotion but of the Church, and if we
come supposing that the words of the Office are to express
our own individual feelings, we shall find them inappropri-
ate, exaggerated, or unreal for they are not the expression of
personal but of communal prayer.

It is the capturing of this communal nature of prayer in
The Office that can give impetus to a priest's prayer and
ministry, difficult though it may be for the solitary priest.
The temptation for the solitary priest at the *Daily Office* is
to slouch in his stall and get through the words as quickly as
possible. Some choose not to say it in the church at all, but
in their study or elsewhere. A concern for physicality can
help. George Herbert in his *A Priest to the Temple*, writes:

> [The priest] when he is to read divine services composeth
> himself to all possible reverence; lifting up his heart and
> hands, and eyes, and using all other gestures which may
> express a hearty and unfeigned devotion. This he doth, first,
> as being truly touched and amazed with the majesty of God
> before whom he then presents himself; yet not as himself
> alone, but as presenting with himself the whole congrega-
> tion....[5]

Michael Ramsey describes it as 'being with God with the
people on your heart'.[6] George Guiver speaks of physical

gestures not merely as optional extras but as important for the present as they have been in history. Such gestures as kneeling, bowing, sitting, standing, making the sign of the Cross. The lectern can be a focus from which to read the lessons and the nave a place in which to focus intercession for the people even when no-one is present. The lighting of the candles; the praying of the *Office* aloud; the singing of the Office along with the psalms and an office hymn; being appropriately dressed in cassock or choir dress; all these can assist in creating an ethos of public prayer that the Church is offering in the office and person of the priest.

Sacred Poetry

In a chapter entitled *Sacred Poetry*[7], Fr Guiver includes psalm, canticle and hymn, for these dominate daily liturgical prayer and, as Henry de Candole has pointed out, 'The psalms formed the nucleus of the Church's Prayers from the earliest Christian days, taken over from the worship of the Jewish Church....'[8] Whilst one must admit that the simplistic way of seeing the psalms as the words of God told through the voice of David—a compendium of the Gospel, encapsulating the mysteries of Christ—may have gone for ever, nevertheless, the actual way that the psalms have worked for people has not changed much. He lists six ways in which our approach to the psalms has remained essentially unaltered.

1. There is a quality of sameness about the psalms. Familiar themes keep returning with the same vocabulary and imagery. This frustrates all desires for stimulation and 'food for thought', 'even though there are times when it "makes you think" '. Guiver points out that this is an aspect of the psalms that has always been there and through this glass darkly we can see the eternal prayer beyond.

2. The psalms have a rhythm which has a capacity to calm us down and make us receptive and can therefore become the first slow paces of prayer.

3. We can respond to the psalms as they stand, because of their concern for some of the most basic elements of human experience that can lead us to tour our subconscious: 'the fear of enemies, desire for revenge, depression, concern with material things, jubilation, victory, glory'. So like a mirror they reflect for us something of our real selves which we can lay before God, using the archetypal imagery of our unconscious and our dreams.

4. The elementary theological nature of the psalms has not changed much.

> As they stand there is no knowledge of Christ.... They circle around an inexorable truth of great simplicity: God and humanity. It is just this passionate relationship with God in all his transcendence which we find so difficult today, and which is probably one of the most important things the Psalms can remind us of.

5. There is also a thematic way of using the psalms; festivals can be enriched by use of appropriate psalms. *Psalm 24* for Ascensiontide, *Psalm 116* for Maundy Thursday, and *Psalm 84* (O How amiable are thy dwellings) for Dedication Festivals. *Psalm 116* (I will lift up the cup of salvation and call upon the name of the Lord) with the Eucharist in mind can be filled out by bringing together this psalm and Eucharistic theme. Similarly *Psalm 121* can exalt and be exalted when used for certain occasions. 'The psalms can have the ability to gather up what we hold out to them and make it expand into a larger space.'

6. There is also a hymnic use of psalms. One can simply sing them like any hymn or song chosen for an occasion.

Finally, a word on the systematic Christian interpretation of the psalms. Here the concern is the praying of the psalms by using them as speaking about Christ (*Ps. 23*), or as being the voice of Christ himself (*Ps. 22*), or being the voice of the Church (*Ps. 126*). It is a New Testament way of using the psalms. The fact that the original author did not intend such a Christian interpretation need not negate this distinctively Christian way of using the psalms. It is simply an acknowledgment of the repetitive patterns in God's way of doing things. Exodus is linked with resurrection, Israel is equated with the Church in a quite legitimate way, 'because they are a repeating pattern in the way things work'. This is a legitimate way of biblical interpretation called typology, which is a matching up of stories and pictures in the history of salvation, on the basis that God's methods remain true to type. While the circumstances and requirements may differ according to the times, the acts of God are seen to follow archetypal patterns. The Suffering Servant passages of Isaiah strike a chord with the Crucifixion of Christ, and the history of Israel and the Church share similar experiences. To quote Guiver:

> ... with typology in the Bible. It does not matter that a Hebrew King entering the Temple to celebrate a victory (*Ps. 118*) knew nothing about the resurrection of Christ. The same God was revealing himself in the same inimitable manner in both events, and both reveal a similar trait in his character, and in the character of his Truth.[9]

While the higher criticism has left us with a predisposition for scientific integrity concerning the origins and reasons for texts, which in itself is good, its negative legacy has to be overcome. Guiver sees a way through this by characterizing the typological interpretation of the psalms in terms of game and the role of the *Daily Office* in terms of game-prayer. This concept of game-prayer he outlines in chapter 5, where he discusses play as being an important element of life, figuring far more importantly than we are prepared to admit. It is a faculty we never lose and takes us into an experience of what becomes real, like children who play at doctors and nurses or cowboys and Indians.

> Our homes are pure theatre. There is no practical need for wallpaper on the walls, or even plaster, but this scenery is essential to the elaborate play which expresses home-life. Even our job, our commitments, the layout of our towns and

their systems of government can all be understood as an
elaborate game, the creation of a world around us which we
need as a framework within which to be ourselves.[10]

The danger arises when we mistake this theatre for serious
reality, rather than a game through which we approach the
truly serious mystery of what it means to be alive and
human. An important point made by Guiver is that modern
Western Society tends to set itself up as a simple goal, rather
than as an elaborate game by confused human creatures
looking for security. Hence the result that the ends of life
become material well-being, security and personal 'freedom'
and the reality which lies below the surface is forgotten.

Game and reality are therefore inseparable and when
separated the result is shallowness. Disaster follows when
there is confusion over which is which. Hence the importance of games in our education, not so much for the kicking
about of an encased ball of air, but for their affective
influence in the way they contribute to character through
self-discipline, relationship and sportsmanship. The most
important discipline is to ensure a fine balance between
game and reality. Similarly, to quote Guiver:

> We can take liturgy so seriously that we have to perform it
> meticulously and correctly, indifferent to whether those
> present are enabled to relate in heart, mind and soul to the
> Lord. We are unable to celebrate it sensitively and release that
> in it which is of the height or depth of joy, sorrow, and all
> that is at the heart of the Christian gospel. We cannot throw
> our whole being into it, because we can only do that when we
> play. Conversely, we can take life as serious reality and see
> liturgy as 'mere' game and therefore only of limited worth.
> Prayer and liturgy fail to be as serious a business as daily life,
> except when they can be connected to its 'real' concerns.
> This, too, leaves us far from the heart of reality.[11]

Guiver's point is that play and serious reality cannot be
separated.

So when Christians celebrate the day's prayers with candles,
flowers, incense, gestures and singing, with the full awareness

that this is a game, and with the intention as far as possible, of playing the game to the full, we are being fools in the best biblical understanding of the term, shaming the serious wisdom of a world which believes it is not playing games, and exulting in play as the most potent means for living life and the gospel to the full.[12]

The point stressed here is the need for utter self-giving in play. Without such commitment all play ends up a shambles. Such self-giving cannot be programmed, it must be spontaneous; the letting-go of all self-consciousness in a self-forgetfulness that abandons oneself to the game. It will begin in diffidence and insecurity, and like prayer, need a persevering courtship before we can feel we are getting anywhere.

But even then, if daily prayer 'feels good', it is not much like our idea of a good game of football. A growing sense of the benefits of the Church's daily worship will always be accompanied by the sense of hard work whose rewards are perceptible but not easy to put one's finger on. For many people it could best be described as a game based on hard work, which only makes sense over a long life-span and within the context of the whole of the life it gradually comes to inform.[13]

The important point is the playing of the game, not the origin of the rules, why it became such a game in the first place, or what difference the evolving shape of the cricket bat makes to cricket today. The typological interpretation of the psalms has to be seen as a serious game. This can be difficult because of our conviction that prayer always has to mean exactly what is being uttered, yet as Guiver says, if this is taken in isolation it can leave us prey to all kinds of pride and self-regard. It has to be balanced by game-prayer which is the role the daily office often fulfils.

Another related problem is the way practices or objects can, with the passage of time, undergo a change of use. Examples could be multiplied from houses to churches, raincoats to chasubles, pictures to the alphabet. While there is a sense in which such knowledge of the evolution of things informs our understanding, it is not always desirable nor necessary to be aware of origins. So it is with the psalms in their daily use, since in different contexts and places they have been used quite differently from the original intention of their author's mind. The recovery of the typological approach may not chime immediately with modern thinking 'but this way of understanding the Psalms and indeed the whole of Scripture is essential if the Church is to stay with the deeper springs of her traditions of prayer'.[14]

Andrew Louth's *Discerning the Mystery*, is concerned with this problem, the roots of which he locates in what Eliot describes as a 'dissociation of sensibility', bequeathed to us by the Enlightenment; 'a dissociation between thought and feeling, between the mind and the heart'.[15] After expounding it in terms of the Enlightenment's legacy, he turns to the Father's use of allegory in the interpretation of Scripture. His SLG pamphlet *Theology and Spirituality* is concerned with the same problem.

I quote Guiver's advice for the Christian interpretation of the psalms:

One good way-in to this is by understanding the first person singular, when it occurs, to refer to the Church. The 'I' who speaks, praises, fears, laments, hopes, is then the Body of Christ, and our voices embody 'the voice of the Bride calling to the Bridegroom'. The psalm now becomes, not the self-preoccupied moanings of an individual, but our prayer with and for the Church, reflecting on her trials and testings, the opposition and misunderstanding she faces, both from without and within, the faith and hope in which she is grounded, and the love and praise which endlessly go forth in the round of worship and prayer. As the subject is plural, concern for the Church's 'self' leaves self-concern behind and becomes a part of love of the brethren, both those people of which she is composed, and those who need yet to receive her message. The Divine Office then becomes in a vivid way what it is, 'the prayer of the Church'. Many of the Psalms can suddenly be revealed in this way as the prayer of Christ in his Body. 'When the Body of the Son prays, the head is not separated from the body. It is the one Saviour of his body, our Lord Jesus Christ, who prays for us, prays in us, and is prayed to by us.'[16]

Such an interpretation is not an act of make-believe. It is an act of the will grounded in theology and in faith, a willing of this meaning, given weight by being shared in space and in time by all those Christians who have brought it to be accepted as a tested way of prayer, emerging at the life-giving behest, they would affirm, of the Holy Spirit.[17]

Proclamation of the Word of God

The proclamation of the Word is an essential ingredient of liturgical prayer and a central feature of the *Office* as well as the *Eucharist*. The Word of God once addressed to our ancestors is addressed to us, and becomes the means whereby the contemporary Church grows in the image and likeness of the God she worships. As the Sacrament has a kerygmatic character, so the Word has a sacramental character, and if this is to be perceived we have to pass beyond a strictly verbal notion of the Word and rediscover its dynamic quality, what Paul Breck describes as 'its revelatory and saving power as an instrument of the divine will'.[18] He quotes from Paul Evdokimov's essay on The Mystery of the Word:

> A sacrament is essentially 'mystical' or spiritual; and yet it is the most concrete act of all, for the liturgical word is filled more than any other with transcendent presence.[19]

Our danger today is to regard the Word as mere inspired text, forgetting that they were first compiled and edited for proclamation in the public liturgical assembly, and found their dynamism and vitality in the event of proclamation, announcement, and address to God's people. The Word of God is to renew, revitalize and re-establish our identity as members of God's people. Central to our experience as the living community of God's people is a divine and living Person in dialogue with his people, in response to whom that community continues to grow as it allows itself to be formed by the living God. Every day is a Day of the Lord when we must listen to his voice and realise that bread alone is not sufficient for daily life, but every word that comes from the mouth of God.

In the Roman Catholic General Instruction on the Liturgy of the Hours, there is the following statement:

> Following ancient tradition, sacred scripture is read publicly in the liturgy not only in the celebration of the Eucharist but also in the Divine Office. This liturgical reading of Scripture is of greatest importance for all Christians.... In liturgical celebrations prayer always accompanies the reading of sacred scripture. In this way the reading may bear greater fruit, and conversely prayer, especially through the psalms, may be more fully developed by the reading and encourage more intense devotion.[20]

The *Daily Office* functions primarily through the medium of the spoken word where hearing and responding to God's Word is mediated and expressed through human speech. It is a good practice to read the Word aloud even when saying the Office alone, because there is a power in speech that can be underestimated. It is a medium in which we articulate our self-giving and through which God is present to us and when in the company of others it makes us present to them. To speak aloud not only gives extra power to the thoughts, emotions and depths of our being which the words articulate. It also objectifies them so that they can be heard more clearly. Speech becomes God's way of giving himself to us and a medium in which we can objectively give ourselves to God. Unspoken thoughts can be so easily forgotten, so that reading aloud can be an effective way of ensuring that the Holy Scriptures which God has caused to be written for our learning may be read, marked, learned and inwardly digested. To quote James White:

> To communicate the corporate memories of the community of faith, its written records—the scriptures—need to be read again and again. The corporate memories contained in scripture give the Church its self-identity. Without the

continual re-iteration of these memories, the Church would simply be an amorphous conglomeration of people of good will but without any real identity. Through the reading and exposition of Scripture, the Christian recovers and appropriates for his or her own life the experiences of Israel and the early Church: escape from slavery, conquest, captivity, hope for a Messiah, incarnation, crucifixion, resurrection, and mission. The Church's survival depends on recapitulating these memories and hopes just as did Israel's. Worship is indeed an 'epiphany of the Church', through the recapitulation of salvation history.[21]

The Lectionary provides a *Lectio continua*, the main purpose being to ensure that virtually the whole of the Bible is read over the year. Such reading does at times synchronize with the Christian Year by providing semi-continuous reading and harmonising with the major Feast Days, Fasts and Seasons, by the provision of relevant reading. This often gives to the scriptural readings and liturgical texts a certain cohesion and subtle relationship integrating with the liturgical season or commemoration being experienced. As the altar is the focus for the Sacrament so the lectern should be the focus for reflecting the dignity of God's Word. Let it be the place from which the Word is read and where it is given a rightful prominence even by the solitary priest at the *Daily Office*. After each reading a period of silence for meditative reflection helps to set a balance between hearing the proclaimed Word and assimilating it.

Prayer

The Lord's Prayer is the core of the *Office*, a prayer in which priest and people are to join, and the significance of this act has its momentary preparation in the Lesser Litany. Addressed to the Blessed Trinity and fixing the object of Christian worship, as well as acknowledging our need of God's mercy we are enabled to offer the *Our Father*. It is uniquely the 'prayer of the faithful,' handed to us when initiated into membership and collecting up the common needs of all to the Father of the Christian family. The Versicles and Responses follow and draw out into particular petitions the implications of the Lord's Prayer. The first is a general petition, the remainder are for the Queen, the clergy, their congregations, for peace and for grace to live well. The nature of this prayer in which priest and people answer to each other emphasizes the sense of common worship.

The Collects, that for the day being primary, links the *Office* with the *Eucharist*, the centre of Christian worship around which the *Offices* circle, reminding us of their dependence on it. A Collect for Peace follows in both offices and then in the morning the third Collect is for the Grace to live well, while in the evening it is one of the Compline Collects for the light of God's presence in our darkness. Our prayer is the Church's response to God's Word, to the revelation of God, which does not return empty but evokes our own response in psalm, canticle and prayer. Our words are the response of his people to God's initiative. To quote the Taizé office:

> The prayer of the Daily Office is part of the praise of the whole creation offered to its Creator. [Our] first and ultimate vocation is to give an intelligible form to this universal praise, and the liturgy of the Church, the Daily Office in particular, expresses this above all.... By the very fact of its existence, creation praises its maker, but this praise needs a spiritual expression.... The Daily Office gives a biblical and universal form to this prayer offered by every Christian in the name of the whole creation.[22]

After the Third Collect

The time immediately following the *Daily Offices* can be for the priest the appropriate moment to extend his prayer in a more personal direction. In the morning, if there is a *Eucharist*, leave thirty minutes for such prayer of quiet waiting before God. A useful way into such prayer is the book *From the Fathers to the Churches*,[23] which provides a daily reading from the Fathers for every day and feast of the year.

'Wherever possible the patristic lessons have been arranged to fit in with the *ASB* lectionary for Morning and Evening Prayer, except on Sundays when more attention has been paid to the theme of the Sunday and thus to the Scriptural lessons appointed for the Eucharist.'[24] There is also a variety of readings from other sources. It can be a way into familiarising oneself with the Fathers, a suggestion that has already been made. Here the spirit of the priest's prayer will be contemplative, and this we shall pick up in the next chapter.

Another useful series of similar daily readings is *The Fourth Lesson*,[25] edited by Campling. While it contains mostly contemporary Christian writing, there is also a selection from the Christian tradition. Its original purpose was to provide a Fourth Lesson of a non-biblical kind to use with the Joint Liturgical Group's *Daily Office*, Series II. The present writer uses it as a non-biblical reading after the *Office* and suggests that other anthologies might be used in the same kind of way. It may be a time for ruminating one's way through one of the Christian classics from the English, Spanish, or German Mystics, and so become an appropriate moment for what is called spiritual reading within the context of the daily prayer that integrates one's devotional life. This appropriate moment after the Third Collect at Evensong can become a way into a more intercessory way of prayer, but still in a spirit of quiet waiting on God. With our great High Priest and Intercessor we wait on God interceding on the world's behalf. Books of *Parish Prayers*, can provide the themes and save the working out of intricate schemes, although a notebook with necessary personal detail can be useful. Let this prayer be more in the form of litany structure rather than collect form. Perhaps over a period of time one might compile one's own book of daily devotions, similar in principle to Lancelot Andrewes' *Private Devotions*. After such evening prayer there may well be another opportunity to swim around in another pool of quiet prayer.

Notes

1. Thomas Merton, *Thoughts in Solitude* (Burns Oates 1975), p. 65.
2. A. Solzhenitsen, from an article by Michael Bourdeaux in *The Christian Century*, 10 February 1971, cited by Howard Williams in *My Word* (SCM 1973), p. 4.
3. Fr Gregory CSWG, *The Divine Office in the Renewal of the Christian Life* (One Tradition Series No. 3).
4. Fr Gregory CSWG, *ibid.*, p. 5.
5. George Herbert, 'A Priest to the Temple' in *Five Pastorals*, edited by Thomas Wood (SPCK 1961), p. 101.
6. Michael Ramsey, *The Christian Priest Today* (SPCK 1972), p. 15.
7. George Guiver CR, *Company of Voices* (SPCK 1988), p. 15.
8. Henry de Candole, *The Church's Prayers* (Mowbray 1953), p. 45.
9. Guiver, *ibid.*, p. 154.
10. Guiver, *ibid.*, p. 31.
11. Guiver, *ibid.*, p. 32.
12. Guiver, *ibid.*, p. 32.
13. Guiver, *ibid.*, p. 32.
14. Guiver, *ibid.*, p. 154.
15. Andrew Louth, *Discerning the Mystery* (Clarendon Press, Oxford 1983), Ch. 1.
16. Augustine's *Exposition of the Psalms, 85(86), 1*.
17. Guiver, *ibid.*, p. 155.
18. Paul Breck, *The Power of the Word* (SVP 1986), p. 15.
19. Paul Evdokimov, *The Mystery of the Word*, cited by Breck, *ibid.*, p. 15.
20. Roman Catholic *General Instruction on the Liturgy of the Hours*. No. 40.
21. James White, *Introduction to Christian Worship*, (Abingdon 1984), pp. 137ff.
22. *The Taizé Office* (Faith Press, London 1966), p. 9.
23. Bro. Kenneth CGA (ed.), *From the Fathers to the Churches* Daily Spiritual Readings (Collins 1983).
24. *Ibid.*, Introduction, p. 8.
25. C. Campling (ed.), *The Fourth Lesson* (DLT 1973), 2 vols.

5

The Priest & Contemplative Living

Life Through Death

In focusing upon what was described earlier as the prayer of quiet waiting upon God my concern is to present it in a much larger context than a mere activity the priest does, and see it as a way of living in prayerful consciousness of the divine presence in whom we already participate, and of whose nature we already partake. Hence the title of this chapter, *The Priest and Contemplative Living*.

In every Christian life—not least that of the priest, the *art of living*, the *ars vivendi* the art of making a radically new start—cannot be practised without an *art of dying*, the *ars moriendi*. Is not life through death the very paradox of the Christian life? This art of dying is by no means an expression of resignation or despair but a constitutive element in the *ars vivendi*, without which neither can be living signs of the Spirit, since it is through this that what is genuinely new emerges and grows, teaching us to make room for new initiatives and institutions of the Spirit. People who have been willing to respond to God in such a *dying and rising* way of living reflect its fruits in their immense humanity in which they are so much at ease with themselves and others; in the strong and confident faith that radiates from them. 'It is doubtful,' writes Michael Ramsey, 'if any of us can do anything at all until we have been very much hurt, and until our hearts have been very much broken'. Earlier it was noted that in his *Apologia*, Gregory of Nazianzen, who had himself experienced 'the despair of being a priest', describes the priest as a servant of God. For him no-one is worthy of God unless he has offered himself completely as a living and holy sacrifice. The suddenness with which his father, the Bishop of Nazianzus, had ordained him priest against his wishes impelled him to flee in terror to Pontus. He had a high conception of the duties of a priest, and was appalled by those around him who were pressing to be priests from worldly motives; love of money, position, power and authority; pushing and thrusting themselves forward, though ignorant of religion and unworthy in their lives. A sense of the difficulties entailed by a cure of souls, by correct theology, by beneficial preaching, overwhelmed him. Inspired by the example of Jonah, whose refusal to preach to the men of Nineveh brought him so many troubles, he returns home. Let us again remind ourselves of what he said to the people of Nazianzus:

> A man must himself be cleansed before cleansing others; himself become wise that he may make others wise; become light before he can give light; draw near to God before he can bring others near; be hallowed before he can hallow them; be possessed of hands before leading others by the hand and wisdom before he can speak wisely.[1]

This kind of inner transformation of which Gregory speaks is the fruit of letting oneself become such a living and holy sacrifice, the art of making a radically new start in the way of the *ars moriendi*. As a runaway priest, his soul was a city of God in violent disorder, and he the unworthy incumbent of the priesthood. When he realized that no-one had a right to resist a call from God so too did he see that one must not anxiously avoid difficulties. On the contrary, on his return to the remote and ugly little town in which he was to exercise his priesthood, described as the least among the townships of Cappadocia and far worse than what is now termed the 'urban desert', he knew he had to go right through the midst of his difficulties and descend to the cause of his terror. For it is there that the greatest chance of meeting God awaits us. 'Whoever wants to save his life, will lose it; and whoever loses it will save it.'

Solitary Refinement

Like Gregory, it is not only one's unworthiness, but also a
sense of one's own inadequacy that consciously—but to a
large extent unconsciously—impels one on one's own journey
to 'Pontus', and tempts one to run away into a spirit of
alienation from reality. In consequence one is led into escape
routes in which one is tempted to hide from the real and
essential task of priesthood. Hence my concern to present
priesthood and prayer as a way of living rather than as a
series of acts. Yet it is a way of living in which the way to
life is through death, an existential disposing of ourselves in
the way of the *Pascha Christi*, so that the death and resurrection of Christ can take hold of one's life and transform it.
Such prayer is not a way of doing something, but a way of
becoming someone. Becoming oneself, one's real self, created
by God, redeemed by the Son and a temple of the Holy Spirit.
The emphasis is on the words *life* and *refinement*, since one
enters a whole new kind of existence, discovering an inner
centre of motivation and love which makes one see oneself
and everything else in a new light.

> Call it faith, (at a more advanced stage) contemplative illumi-
> nation, call it the sense of God or even mystical union. All
> these are different aspects or levels of the same kind of
> realization, the awakening of ourselves to a new kind of
> awareness in Christ, created in Him, redeemed by Him, to be
> transformed and glorified in and with Him. In Blake's words
> 'the doors of perception are opened' and all life takes on a new
> meaning; the real sense of our own existence, which is normally
> veiled and distorted by the routine distractions of an alienated
> life, is now revealed in a central intuition. What was lost and
> dispersed in the relative meaninglessness and triviality of
> purposeless behaviour (living like a machine, pushed around by
> impulsions and suggestions from others), is brought together in
> a fully conscious integrated significance. According to the
> Christian Tradition, this peculiar and brilliant focus is the

work of love and the Holy Spirit. This 'loving knowledge' which sees everything transfigured 'in God', coming from God and working for God's creative redemptive love and tending to fulfilment in the glory of God, is a contemplative knowledge, a fruit of living and realizing faith, a gift of the Spirit.[2]

Such contemplative refinement of life takes one across the abyss that lies between reason and vision, between knowledge about things and immediate perception of things. Too often one's response to God can be conditioned within a propositional framework, leaving one's response so incomplete because it has been so narrowly rational, a life lived on the basis of concepts.

St Gregory the Great and the Pastoral Rule

In the sixth century Gregory the Great was the first to lay down the master principles that should govern the life of the pastor. His *Pastoral Rule*, originally intended for bishops and translated by King Alfred, became the textbook of the medieval episcopate. It is however equally applicable to all pastors of souls and has become so, ranking with the *Apologia* of Gregory of Nazianzen, to whom he acknowledges his indebtedness, and Chrysostom's *On the Priesthood*, as one of the classics on the priestly life. All three are *apologies* for wishing to shun the office of priest or bishop by describing the responsibilities involved in such a dignity.

Our concern is with what Gregory has to say about the place of contemplation in the life of the pastor of souls. Contemplation for Gregory is not something to be confined to a select few, a spiritual élite. It is not surprising to find therefore that some of his principal expositions of the contemplative life are in the homilies he preached to mixed congregations in the Lateran Basilica. In his *Homily on Ezekiel* he says:

If therefore there is no state of life of the faithful from which the grace of contemplation can be excluded, anyone who keeps his heart within him, may also be illumined by the light of contemplation, so that no one can glory in this grace as if it were singular.[3]

Among disqualifications for the pastoral office he names 'ignorance of the light of heavenly contemplation.' In *The Pastoral Rule* he writes:

> Let not the pastor diminish his care of things within through his occupation about things without; nor forsake the oversight of things without through his anxiety about things within; lest either being given up to things external he fall away within; or being occupied solely with internal matters he fail to pay that which is due to his neighbours abroad.[4]

He considers an admixture of the contemplative life to be a condition of the fruitful performance of the pastoral office, and he took it for granted that all pastors of souls may, and should, exercise contemplation. He warns about rejoicing in the pressure of 'worldly commotions' so that one becomes ignorant of those inward things which one ought to have taught others. This is because, he points out, when this happens the life of those under us becomes without doubt benumbed, and such of the flock as desire to make spiritual progress find themselves stumbling at the example of him set over them, the pastor being the very stumbling block in their path.

> For when the head languishes, the members have no vigour. It is in vain that an army, seeking contact with the enemy, hurries behind its leader, if he has lost the way. No exhortation then uplifts the minds of subjects, no reproof castigates their faults, for when one who is a spiritual guardian fulfils the office of a judge of the world, the shepherd's care of the flock is lacking; and subjects cannot see the light of the truth, for when earthly cares occupy the pastor's mind, dust, driven by the winds of temptation, blinds the eyes of the Church.[5]

His advice to preachers is that their goal should be to imitate Christ and that they should aim at the two lives, the union of the active and contemplative, for:

Whosoever opens his mind in holy works, has over and above to extend it to the secret pursuits of inward contemplation. For he is no perfect preacher who either from devotion to contemplation neglects works that ought to be done, or from urgency in business puts aside the duties of contemplation.[6]

The purpose of such contemplative living is not mere identification with things invisible, but that, through a life lived constantly in the midst of unseen realities, our identification with the flock goes beyond acts of service and the expression of sympathetic thoughts in the moments of their difficulties. Our sympathy and love as pastors, our joy and long-suffering, our kindness and endurance, are to be a condition of life we share with them, that the pastor may:

... by the bowels of his kindness transfer to himself the infirmity of others and by the height of contemplation be carried beyond himself in his desire for things invisible; that he may neither while he seeketh things on high, despise the weakness of his neighbour; nor being suited to the weakness of his neighbour abandon the desire for things on high.[7]

In the *Morals* Gregory points out that they who bear themselves well in authority are those:

... who lay aside at intervals the din of earthly business for the love of God, and there in the secrets of their hearts they put aside the tumult of temporal activities, and at the summit of their contemplation search out the sentence of the divine will.... For in order that they engage in outward employments without injury to themselves they constantly take care to withdraw to the secrets of their heart.[8]

Knowing God

Today many people are thirsting for a knowledge of God but it is for an experience and understanding that is far more than a concept that concludes an argument. The contemporary French Orthodox theologian Olivier Clément has said that there is a thirst for a living knowledge of the Trinity and the need for our Age is for a truly Trinitarian paternity—'a fatherhood lived in brotherly respect for the other so that the life-giving Spirit may be communicated'[9] Gregory argues that:

> [Such] inward knowledge is not cognizable unless there is a cessation from outward embarrassments... if we wish to contemplate things within, let us rest from outward engagements. The voice of God is heard when, with minds at ease, we rest from the bustle of this world and the divine precepts are pondered by us in the deep silence of the heart.[10]

To know God in this way is to know him as more than an idea in the mind, and implies a knowing of God in the true sense of the root meaning of 'know', which is to become one with the object of our knowing. In this way our knowing passes beyond 'knowledge about' to 'experience of' the very reality and presence of God the Blessed Trinity in the depths of our hearts. Such a personal experience and discovery of the Blessed Trinity is nothing less than a living awareness of the dogma expressing a revealed truth. One does not assimilate it to one's mode of understanding but allows it to effect a profound change, an inner transformation of the spirit that enables one to experience it mystically.[11] F.D. Maurice had this kind of experience—a disclosure of God the Blessed Trinity in whom he was then baptized—and it transformed his life. Subsequently, this 'sense of God', or in Gregory's words, this 'inward knowledge', became the basis and presupposition of all his thinking about God. He was then able to see the doctrine of the Trinity to be the ground of all society—the only ground of universal fellowship, the only idea of a God of love without which men would be divided from each other.[12]

Such a life-giving experience and discovery of God is the fruit of prayer; it is not an optional extra in our thinking, but the very womb in which that thought is conceived in a deep experience of the heart. As Fr Allchin points out, it is here that we discover something of the 'Godness of God', his utter transcendence, his unique immanence at the heart of our being. Such 'inward knowledge', knowing God interiorly, is to discover a presence that is spontaneously shared, the essence of prayer. One cannot help being affected by such experienced prayer that stimulates the growth of awe and adoration and one's absolute dependence on God. At the same time it is soon realized that this 'sense of God' is something which cannot be brought into the orbit of investigation and control by the understanding, nor can it be encompassed or trapped in a concept. It cannot be used or controlled by us. One must not cling to Him, intellectually, spiritually, or psychologically. One must allow the experience to change one in the direction of its demand for a radical change of heart in the way of *ars moriendi*. This brings renewed vision, a readiness to see and think in a new way, which takes one beyond the normal structures of human thought and knowledge, because God is beyond all concepts we can form of Him. The experience will have iconoclastic effects as it topples one's idols of God, the illusions one has about oneself, and the world in which one lives. God's call will be to reform one's habitual ways of thinking and avoid the temptation of the intellect to adapt the mysteries of the wisdom of God to human ways of thought. The fruit of such inner personal experience is the revelation of the givenness of God, the 'inward knowledge' of which Gregory speaks.

Gregory would be the first to deny that such a way of knowing God can be open only to a spiritual élite and that the path towards it is a lonesome individual journey. Christian prayer is never a flight of the alone to the *Alone*. Our relationship with God is a covenant relationship mediated through our membership of the community of God's people, the Church, and is the common experience of the mysteries of faith which is open to all Christians. The Russian mystic, Theophan the Recluse, tells us that the person who turns to God and is sanctified by the sacraments, immediately receives feeling towards God within himself, which from this moment begins to lay the foundation in his heart for the ascent on high. He goes on:

Because all have grace, only one thing is necessary; to give grace free scope to act. Grace receives free scope to act in so far as the ego is crushed and the passions uprooted. The more our heart is purified, the more lovely becomes our feeling towards God... those who commit themselves irrevocably towards grace will pass under its guidance as it shapes and forms them in a way known only to itself.[13]

This is what will, in itself, clear the mind of its darkness and restore it to that contact with God in himself, which can be described as true theology or true prayer, which is effectively the same thing. When Anselm of Canterbury first expressed, 'God is that than which nothing greater can be thought', it was the intellect giving expression to what he had experienced in prayer and worship. Apparently at Bec he had been exercising all the abilities of his mind to discover the rationale of the nature of God. Suddenly, 'one night during mattins the grace of God shone in his heart, the whole matter became clear to his mind, and a great joy and jubilation filled his whole being.'[14] Sister Benedicta goes on:

It was a matter of illumination about what was already believed, and it is this that provided the starting point for his arguments, not the reverse. It happened in the middle of a monastic service, and the whole setting of it is a prayer of longing and desire for God which is entirely monastic in tone. There is a joy and excitement which is far removed from the logical demonstrations of scholasticism and closer to the mystical experience of prayer.[15]

So Anselm can say 'Thank you good Lord, for by your gift I first believed, and now by your illumination I understand.' It is the fruit of that spirit of prayer in which the *Proslogion* opens.

> Enter the chamber of your soul,
> Shut everything out except God
> And that which can help you in seeking him,
> And when you have shut the door seek him.
> Now my whole heart, say to God,

'I seek your face,
Lord it is your face I seek.'[16]

Disposition

This brings us to the point with which we began, that 'The
climax of purity is the beginning of theology', and to the
points raised in the second chapter. It is only the pure in
heart who see God, and prayer precedes purity just as purity
precedes vision, and vision precedes theology. To enter into
this kind of 'inward knowledge' and thereby discover an
inner centre of motivation and love, within which one sees
oneself and everything else in a new light, requires both the
rooting of the whole person in the experience of worship and
prayer, and the placing of oneself unconditionally at the
disposal of God. Such 'inward knowledge' and the disposition of coming to God unconditionally are closely linked.
'Unconditional' implies a willingness to be stripped of the
'hang-ups' that push and impel and prevent one from being
free, the intellectual hang-ups of one's philosophical presup-
positions, and the psychological hang-ups that rattle like
dried skeletons in the cupboards of one's memory. There are
also the spiritual hang-ups in the 'sins that do so easily beset
us.'

Such hang-ups veil and distort the real sense of existence,
impelling and pushing one like a machine into the agitation
of spirit and the triviality of purposeless behaviour. They
become the masks with which to hide from God, because of
the fear of appearing before him naked. Yet to stand and
wait before God in the silence of utter nakedness, beyond the
barricades of one's inadequacies, is what coming before God
unconditionally implies. We submit ourselves to this process
because it is the only way to listen with God. 'The voice of
God is heard', says Gregory, 'when with minds at ease, we
rest from the bustle of the world and the divine precepts are
pondered by us in the deep silence of the heart.'[17] It is a
silence embracing not only the conscious levels of our being
but the unconscious as well.

In this silence we discover that most of the bustle and noise is within oneself. A kind of 'inner warfare' explodes into our consciousness revealing the extent of the lack of peace in our own hearts, expressing itself not only in the agitated condition of body and senses, but also in the conscious and sub-conscious levels of mind and spirit. These are the noises that fragment and distract one's spirit, the things that bump one awake in the night in the anxieties and worries of agitating thoughts and desires, and in the tensions between the pain of real life and the imagined joy one's fantasies and dreams bring. Alongside these are the people one finds difficult to relate to, the things on one's conscience and the conflicts and tensions on the emotional level. This kind of noise distracts and diffuses our prayer.

In the fourth century the Abba Isaac told this to John Cassian and his friend Germanus when they asked him to teach them to pray. He said:

> The mind at prayer is as it was made to be before the time of prayer. When we dispose ourselves to prayer, the image of the same actions, words and feelings, will flit before our eyes, and reproducing what has gone before, will make rise in us either feelings of anger or depression or will cause us to go over again past desires or business.[18]

If God is to reveal himself in the depths of our being, and we are to hear God in Gregory's sense, then we must flee from noise through both interior and exterior silence. 'Whatever we would not have our minds entertain when we are at prayer,' says Abba Isaac, 'let us before the hour of prayer hasten to expel from the secret places of our hearts.'[19] Herein St Basil tells us, is the beginning of the purified heart, the necessary precondition for seeing God.

Such quiet waiting on God helps us to grow into a condition of tranquillity in which all inordinate movements and desires, passions and thoughts are quelled, enabling us to be more ready to listen and know God. In such stillness and tranquillity one surrenders oneself totally to God, dwelling and revealing himself in this temple of God which is my

body. It is a prayer in which one passes beyond one's
normal habit of reasoning about God and one's duties
towards him, to discover that, as one opens oneself beyond
the hang-ups that have hitherto compelled one, we come
face-to-face with God the iconoclast whose presence
instantly destroys our idols. In the words of C.S. Lewis to
Malcolm:

> Only God himself can let the bucket down into the
> depths of us. And on the other side he must constantly
> work as the iconoclast. Every idea of him we form, he
> must in mercy shatter. The most blessed result of
> prayer would be to rise thinking, 'But I never knew
> before, I never dreamed....' I suppose it was at such a
> time that Thomas Aquinas said of all his theology 'It
> reminds me of straw.'[20]

The priest must build within himself the type of cell where
solitude reigns, an inner chamber in which tranquillity is
experienced. Here is where he comes face to face with his
true self and God in an unconditional nakedness, open,
receptive, and without preconceived ideas of what God the
Blessed Trinity will reveal. In this place of solitude one
waits beyond the barricades in stillness, ready to meet God
on his terms and hoping to receive him as he wishes to
make himself known. Here feeding on the thoughts of the
heart, we discover the truth that sets us free, not as an
object of knowledge to be possessed, but as the Truth in
the person of the Blessed Trinity by whom we are possessed. He it is who frees us in a salvation which is more
than forgiveness; He it is whose freely given gift is the
genuine renewal of our whole being. We inwardly experience the mystery of living in the Trinity; a mutual indwelling in love; a love shared between the Divine persons and
ourselves. The Spirit, says St Irenaeus, comes to seize us
and give us to the Son, and the Son gives us to the Father.
'If anyone loves me we will come to him and make in him
our abode.'

The Poverty of the Single Verse

In the stillness and silence in which God spontaneously shares his presence with us, John Cassian advises the helpful practice of using a single short phrase in which to focus one's prayer. 'The mind thus casts out and represses the rich and ample matter of all thoughts and restricts itself to the poverty of the single verse.'[21]

'Be still and know that I am God' (*Psalm 46 v. 10*) is a verse which is often used. It should be repeated over and over again, faithfully, lovingly, continuously. The sole sound will be the sound of this phrase, rather like a harmonic within, building up a resonance that leads us forward to our own wholeness. In the slow and deliberate repetition of this verse we hold ourselves still in the realization of the presence of God in Christ. Instead of thinking about him or trying to see him refracted through our imagination, we brood on the truth that he actually is present to us and nearer to us than the air we breathe, letting the heart and mind become absorbed in attending to this stupendous truth, that he is as present to us as he was to his first followers. Our prayer is more than attention to this truth of God's presence, it is an experience of it in which the self is quite forgotten. Our consciousness becomes like that on which we have 'gazed' and obedient to that to which we have 'listened', as we become one in a union of love with the subject of our knowing. Thereby, our knowledge passes beyond knowledge about to that inward knowledge which is nothing less than an experience of the very reality and presence of God in the heart.

Here we open in receptivity and obedience, listening rather than giving, commanding or speaking. It is not a passive condition, but a consciousness; a realisation that our acts do not originate in ourselves, but are drawn out and inspired by acts of God. Such inspiration will effect in us a radical change of heart and mind which brings new vision. Yet this will only happen in so far as we are willing to die in order that we might live. For the experience, in so far as there is nothing blocking our response, cleanses and awakens our adoration and love, so that resolutions are not needed. Our consciousness, awakened and touched by this living Presence, receives from him an infusion of life, that issues spontaneously in thoughts and acts rising from this change of feeling in this communion of prayer.

> Be at peace with your own soul, enter eagerly into the treasure house that is within you and so you will see the things that are in heaven; for there is but one single entry to them both. The ladder that leads to the kingdom is hidden within your soul. Flee from sin, dive into yourself and in your soul you will discover the stairs by which to ascend.[22]

A Life, Not a Technique

The essence of what is written here is that prayer is neither a technique, a theory or a method, but is rather a way of life at the centre of which is God the Blessed Trinity, a life centred in him, a life that is caught from constant nearness to him. Such prayer, in which the continual recollection of the holy Presence of God is primary, is therefore a disposition of life rather than the perfect performance of a technique. This life is rooted in the sacraments and centred in the liturgy; a Eucharistic life, in which one disposes oneself towards God through Christ Jesus that the prayer of Jesus might arise in our hearts. This was the spirit of Abba Isaac's advice to John Cassian. He did not introduce him to some predetermined doctrine and practice, but to a way of life that was to be caught from constant nearness to God in the continual recollection of his Presence. Hence Cassian can say that our practical perfection depends on first knowing the nature of our faults, and secondly, finding out the order of the virtues and forming our characters by striving to perfect ourselves in them.[23]

It is here that the *Pascha Christi* must be allowed to take hold on one's life to transform it. In the way of *ars moriendi*, one must lose one's life in order to find it in the

emptying out of unreality and artificiality that becomes the
ars vivendi. One lays down one's life in the poverty of the
single verse, 'letting-go' of everything, that in the poverty of
one's spirit one might see the Kingdom of God. Tito
Colliander explains it like this.

> You should see yourself as a child who is setting out to learn
> the first sounds of letters, and who is taking his first tottering
> steps. All worldly wisdom and all the skills you have are
> totally worthless in the warfare that awaits you, and equally
> without value are your social standing and your possessions.
>
> Property that is not used in the Lord's service is a burden
> and knowledge that does not engage the heart is barren and
> therefore harmful because presumptuous. It is called naked,
> for it is without warmth and fosters no love.
>
> You must thus abandon your knowledge and become a
> dunce in order to become wise; you must become a pauper in
> order to be rich and a weakling if you wish to be strong.[24]

Our search is for the true self and the experience of our
own personal and infinite capacity to be known and loved by
God. The real self lies beyond all selfishness, and can only
be known in God as part of that 'inward knowledge.' To
arrive at it, one must enter into a radical experience of
personal poverty in the surrendering of the false image that
one has come to regard as one's true self, along with all the
unreality this has created in one's own life. Discovering that
one is not what one imagined oneself to be is a painful
experience. The pain being in proportion to the extent that
we have taken the illusions to be real. All such artificiality
crumbles as one concentrates, attends and waits on God,
whose light of truth illuminates the true self, filling one not
only with a sense of nothingness before the beauty of God,
but bringing the kind of brokenness in spirit, the contrite
heart of the poor in spirit which is a blessing, the kingdom
of heaven within them.

In St Augustine's language we have found the essential
'stepping stone' that will lead us to God, in the real self
which becomes the sacrifice of our broken and contrite heart
that we know God will not despise. The silence into which

God calls us is an interior condition of humility and poverty, beyond what normally conditions us in the senses, emotions and affections, so that we may be free to say 'yes' to him with our very being. Such an experience goes beyond mere words, pious phrases, and sentiments, beyond thought itself. God calls us to rest and 'taste' in a condition of living communion with him in the continuous response of our being. Then the words of T.S. Eliot ring true, that:

> Prayer is more
> Than an order of words, the conscious occupation
> Of the praying mind, or the sound of the voice praying.[25]

It is looking upon God in pureness of heart, rather like a baby looking on his father's or mother's face. It certainly is as natural as that. A waiting and looking and resting in the security of an experience—the experience of one's whole being 'tasting' the very presence of the beloved whose love meets one in an embrace of peace. Just as there is dialogue between mother and baby in their loving embrace—a dialogue not of words but of love—so too in this high point of prayer one is defined by our dialogue with God. Yet this dialogue should not be seen in terms of a banal conversation, but rather in terms of being held in the loving embrace of God; communicating a life that words would only faintly express. One is drawn into an assimilation with God that convinces one that no longer does one live to oneself, but that God lives in one and one lives in God. 'Eye has not seen, nor ear heard... nor has it entered into the heart of man to conceive what God has prepared for those who love him.'

New psychic and spiritual powers blossom forth, released through the energies of God that have touched one's consciousness. One passes over the abyss that lies between merely thinking and actually seeing, between knowledge about things and immediate perception of things. Such 'inward knowledge' is different from the knowledge our minds bring to us, being the fruit of letting ourselves be possessed by God in an experience in which we intuitively know that God loves us. It brings healing, consolation and

peace, restores our strength and gives a child-like trust, joy
and peace in the embrace of the indwelling Trinity. Such a
sense of God becomes the presupposition of all one's
thinking.

Conversion and New Life

So we return full circle to Gregory Nazianzen and the words
quoted earlier:

> ... no-one is worthy of the mightiness of God, and the sacri-
> fice, and the priesthood, who has not first presented himself
> to God, a living, holy sacrifice, and set forth the reasonable
> well-pleasing service, and sacrificed to God the sacrifice of
> praise and the contrite spirit, which is the only sacrifice
> required of us by the Giver of all; how could I dare to offer
> to Him the external sacrifice, the antitype of the great mys-
> teries, or clothe myself with the garb and name of priest,
> before my hands had been consecrated by holy works; before
> my eyes had been consecrated to gaze safely upon created
> things, with wonder only for the Creator, and without injury
> to the creature; before my ear had been sufficiently opened to
> the instruction of the Lord, and he had opened my ear to
> hear... a wise man's word in an obedient ear; before my
> mouth had been opened to draw in the Spirit, and opened
> wide to be filled with the spirit of speaking mysteries and
> doctrines; and my lips bound, to use the words of wisdom by
> divine knowledge... before my feet had been set upon the
> rock... and my footsteps directed in a godly fashion....[26]

The illumination Gregory sees as the prime necessity of
the priest, comes, when like him the priest begins with
himself and investigates the possibilities of conversion and
new life. Our moment of illumination is born when we offer
our whole being to knowing the Truth which is beyond concepts, and then receive it as a transfiguring and converting
experience. The new life of priesthood and contemplation is
to be a perpetual conversion, a refinement in solitude, a
turning from the kingdom of sin and alienation, towards the
Kingdom of God and union with him.

A primary part of the framework of that total life of conversion is the *Liturgy in Eucharist and Daily Office*. Our Liturgy is what John Wesley called 'a converting ordinance' wherein we proclaim the fact of God's redeeming work, and so become more and more identified with it. Furthermore, it is a framework of prayer based on Word and Sacrament, and so prevents us from introducing any antipathy between liturgical prayer and other aspects of prayer. Walter Hilton helps us avoid the error of thinking in terms of progressive development from one to the other. He sees such development as a growth in delight with which one enters into whatever form of prayer is appropriate at the time, for they are all entrances into the eternal prayer of Jesus.

The Psalter

In giving oneself to the prayer of contemplation the *Bible* and the *Psalter* will become more immediately alive with meaning. The point has already been made that the way of contemplation can never be an individualistic and esoteric experience outside the community of faith. In the *Liturgy of Office and Eucharist*, our participation in Word and Sacrament will provide the living context in which we proclaim the fact of God's redeeming work and become more and more identified with it. The contemplative spirit of our closeness to God while it has a personal dimension, must always be rooted in the *sui generis* experience of the Church.

The Psalter will be our prayer book *par excellence*. Increasing numbers of people are beginning to rediscover the psalms and are using them in their solitary prayer. Their familiar recurring phrases shape the sub-conscious as well as the conscious mind and create the interior attitudes of repentance and need. Using them in this way leads to the discovery of the richness of this deeply human prayer-book, where the failure of man and his condition is brought to the mercy and faithfulness of God. The two themes running through the

Psalter, the glory of God in praise and thanksgiving and the need of man in the penitential psalms, find their conjunction in us through Baptism and are therefore brought into the wholeness of reconciliation in Christ. Reciting the psalms daily and using them contemplatively directly effects our own conversion—our understanding of our need for God's love—contributes to our life in Christ, not always consciously, but as the underlying ground of our prayer.[27]

John Cassian in his *Conference X* gives a clue to the contemplative use of the psalms. Here he advises the practice of using the single short phrase to achieve the stillness necessary for prayer. A daily reading of the psalms should not only feed and identify the heart and mind with the statements of the Psalter, but at the same time should provide a fund of single verses upon which to ruminate in times of contemplative stillness. The purpose of the single verse is to bring us to the realization that in essence our aim is to so dispose ourselves that the prayer of Jesus arises in our hearts. So the verse must not only be in our heart at those times when one consciously enters into contemplative stillness, but says Cassian, 'must always be in the heart, till having been moulded by it you grow accustomed to repeat it even in your sleep. On rising it should anticipate all your waking thoughts, and throughout the day it should be singing ceaselessly in the recesses of your heart.'[28] Such prayer is to allow God's mysterious and silent presence within us to become more and more the reality which gives meaning and shape and purpose to all we do, to everything we are.

Carl Jung was once asked in an interview whether he believed in God. After a pause he quietly said, 'No, I know.' Cassian touches on this reality of direct experience as the fruit of contemplation. He tells us that in reading the psalms we no longer just read them or memorise them. We come to get at their meaning not by reading the text, but by experiencing and anticipating it. This is the essence of what Thomas Merton says of the Saints and Fathers, who did not simply consider the psalm as they passed over it, drawing from it pious reflection, but entered into the action of the psalm and allowed themselves to be absorbed in the spiritual agony of the psalmist and of the God whom he represented. They allowed their sorrows to be swallowed up in the sorrows of this mysterious Personage, and found themselves swept away on the strong tide of his hope into the very depths of God. He goes on to say that we too find out that, when we bring our own sorrows and desires and hopes and fears to God and plunge them all into the sorrows and hopes of the mysterious One who sings the psalm, a kind of transubstantiation is effected. We have put all that we have or rather all our poverty, all that we have not, into the hands of Christ. He who is Everything and has everything pronounces over our gift words of his own. Consecrated by contact with the poverty he assumed to deliver us, we find that in his poverty our poverty becomes infinite riches; in his sufferings our defeats are transubstantiated into victories and his death becomes our everlasting life.[29]

The Bible

What John Cassian says about the psalms, getting at their meaning not by reading the text but by experiencing and anticipating it, is similar to what he says about Holy Scripture. The sense of Scripture is revealed not by a commentary, but by what he calls practical proof, because our own experience exposes what he calls the very veins and marrow of the Word of God. Hence the Bible stands alongside the Psalter as the reservoir that will irrigate our prayer. In private and corporate reading of Scripture, the words can be sacramental as we recall God's mighty acts in the history of salvation, the history of his people. We are standing before God making *anamnesis*, remembrance, and giving thanks for what he has done, and the element of conversion is not absent as we read of the long return to the Father accomplished by the People of God in the Old and New Testaments, and which must be accomplished in each Christian. The acts of God's mercy are read, the need of man is

acknowledged, and this is the vital part of the accomplish-
ment of the mystery of Christ in each one of us.

The problem of interpretation is not the finding of some
key with which to extract from the Word of Scripture, either
some particular doctrine or the meaning of the Gospel for
today. Rather does it rest on the faith of the Church that in
the Scriptures God speaks to his Church. The faith which the
Scriptures express, and which the Church offers us and to
which she leads us, kindles the light of the Holy Spirit in the
heart of the believer. The Scriptures are part of the Tradition,
which does not hold the Church captive to the past, but is
something in which the Christian must live and move as the
surest guide to the future. The Scriptural Tradition is no
formula, no form of words, but a continuity of life, mystical
and sacramental, the mystery of Christ to which the Scriptures bear witness. Herein is the *Rule of Faith* which defines
the Church and in accordance with which the Scripture must
be interpreted. At the heart of the Faith is a mystery that is
lived, a continuity of life that claims the whole man. The
apprehension of this mystery is not simply a cerebral
activity, but comes in ways that are unfathomable. This is
because the mystery draws out our faith and love. The
mystery is Christ, so it is not just a question of believing the
right things, not even simply of hearing the Word of Christ,
but more deeply it is a question of being with him at the
deepest level in prayer. 'He who truly possesses the word of
Jesus,' says Ignatius of Antioch, 'can also hear his stillness,
that he may be perfect, that he may act through what he
says, that he may be known through his silence.'

'Before any articulation of our confession of Christ,'
writes Andrew Louth, 'there is an inarticulate closeness to
Christ, to that creative silence out of which the Word comes,
to that stillness in which are wrought the mysteries that cry
out.'[30] We do not subordinate Scripture to the articulated
faith of the Church, but listen to Scripture from a contemplative stillness that is being with Christ. This is something
given and known in the life of the Church and in the
Tradition which is the movement of the Spirit in the Church.

Such a contemplative approach to Scripture is not only found in the Fathers, but also in such mystics as Aelred of Rievaulx, Richard of St Victor, St Bernard and others. These men lived in a Scriptural atmosphere, and being saturated with the spirit of the Bible, their thoughts were moulded by it. By constant communion of heart and mind with the Divine presence, they attained a deeply religious understanding of man's problems and the divine plan of salvation. Their spiritual insight into Scripture discovered the sacred history of the human race and the soul's spiritual journey, and they recognized there the soul's ascent to God. They drank from the divine well-spring and so read the Bible under the Spirit who inspired it. This explains why they could discover, as if by instinct, the true meaning of the text, for their minds were spontaneously in tune with the thought of the sacred books. They lived the reality which their exegesis sought to discover behind the words.[31]

Within this contemplative approach to Scripture is the conviction that Scripture allows of allegorical interpretation. In the spirit of St Paul, who contrasts shadow and reality, for such writers the sole reality is Christ and him we know through love. All else therefore is shadow, is allegory, and has value only in so far as it makes manifest the truth of the mystery of Christ. This recognizes the fact that Scripture does not contain the whole truth, but only a partial reflection of it through which we might be enabled to discern the truth itself. Allegory is appropriate because it is not a definite method yielding clear and predictable results, but helps us to discern through Scripture a truth not contained in Scripture but witnessed to by it. In Scripture the truth is broken up so that we can grasp it and receive it as a gift and then look beyond it to the Giver, to Christ who is Truth.

Such an approach to Scripture is not scientific in the strict sense, but it is not meant to be. It does however have its canons of procedure. It is contemplative, it is a way of prayer, a living encounter of a life rooted in the mystery of Christ, therefore it is not a simple matter of Scriptural exposition but much more. At a deeper level it is a matter of discernment, an alertness to the Word's disclosure of himself through this engagement with Scripture. Here we seek to see Scripture as a witness pointing to the Word—to Jesus Christ, in whose presence we live in the Spirit—as it seeks to take us beyond the text to someone who could be captured by no text, to our Lord himself. The task of listening to God in Scripture, which is prayer, is a listening to the Word speaking to us through Scripture, rather than piecing together some fragmentary witness of Scripture to make some construction of our own. In the end we pass beyond our own efforts; we let go our intellect and what we spin from it and simply listen.

We are not surrendering our reason to some arbitrary human convention. We are brought to the meaning of Scripture, which is the mystery of Christ revealing the Father, not by our own ingenuity but by the Spirit. The understanding of Scripture is not a purely human affair. The whole of revelation would be negated if the Spirit who inspired the prophets and apostles did not also move the hearts of believers to recognize and obey the Word of God speaking to them through their writings.

This contemplative approach to Scripture in an openness to allegory is but an openness to God—to God's manifestation of himself in Scripture—so that we are responding to the mystery to which it is a witness. From this openness springs our apprehension of dogma and doctrine, the articulation of that stillness in the closeness of the mystery of Christ. Fr George Moloney sums up the message of contemplation in these words:

> ... to the degree that one has purified and disciplined himself to sit before the Lord and listen to his Word, to that extent he can stand before the world and witness to the Word in loving service... it teaches us the need to become prophets of the Word; meditating on the Word spoken in Scripture and re-lived in the mystery of the indwelling Trinity, we are sent forth as witnesses to that same existential Word being spoken in the world, as we yield ourselves to the process of bringing forth that Word in its fullness.[32]

This is the new life that is needed by the world as it is by the Church. It is a life that is self-authenticating because it has its origin in a vision, the vision which is the fruit of the contemplative's prayer:

> Enkindle within us the fire of your love
> And thou shalt renew the face of the earth.

Notes

1. Gregory Nazianzen, *In Defence of his Flight to Pontus,* Nicene and Post-Nicene Fathers, Second Series, Vol. VII, Oration II, 71 p. 219.

2. Thomas Merton, *Contemplation in a World of Action* (Doubleday Image Book 1973 New York), p. 176.

3. Gregory the Great, *Homily on Ezekiel* II, vv. 19, 20.

4. Gregory the Great, *Pastoral Rule*, II, vii, Benedictine Text trans. H.R. Bramley (Parker & Co. Oxford and London 1874), p. 89, where I have replaced the word 'ruler' with 'pastor'.

5. Gregory the Great, *ibid.*, p. 91.

6. Gregory the Great, *Morals* XXVIII.56.

7. Gregory the Great, *Pastoral Rule* II.v.

8. Gregory the Great, *Morals* XXVIII.33.

9. Olivier Clément, cited in *The Kingdom of Love and Knowledge* (DLT 1979) by A.M. Allchin, p. 6.

10. Gregory the Great, *Morals* V.55.

11. V. Lossky, *The Mystical Theology of the Eastern Church* (James Clarke 1973), p. 6.

12. A.M. Allchin, *ibid.*, p. 6.

13. Theophane the Recluse in *The Art of Prayer*, trans. Kadloubovsky and Palmer (Faber, 1966), p.59.

14. Sr Benedicta Ward SLG, *Anselm of Canterbury, A Monastic Scholar* (Fairacres Pamphlet 1977), p. 9.

15. Sr. Benedicta, *ibid.*

16. Jasper Hopkins and Herbert Richardson (ed. & trans.), *Anselm of Canterbury,* ch. 1 'Proslogion—Arousing the Mind for Contemplating God'.

17. Gregory the Great, *Morals* XXIII.37.

18. Cassian, *Conference* IX.3 (Abbot Isaac I) p. 388, Nicene and Post-Nicene Fathers, 2nd series, Vol. XI.

19. Cassian, *ibid.*
20. C.S. Lewis, *Letters to Malcolm,* (Bles 1964), p. 84.
21. Cassian, *Conference* X.11, *ibid.*, p. 407.
22. Isaac of Nineveh, cited in *The Art of Prayer*, p. 164.
23. Cassian, *Conference* IX.2 (Abbot Isaac I), p. 387.
24. Tito Colliander, *The Way of the Ascetics* (Hodder and Stoughton 1960), p. 24.
25. T.S. Eliot, Little Gidding, *The Four Quartets.*
26. Gregory of Nazianzen, *ibid.*, p. 223.
27. Sr.Benedicta Ward, *Liturgy Today* (Fairacres Pamphlet 34, 1974).
28. Cassian, *Conference* X.10 (Abbot Issac 2) *ibid.*, p. 405.
29. Thomas Merton, *Bread in the Wilderness,* (Catholic Book Club 1953), p. 66.
30. Andrew Louth, *The Hermeneutical Question Approached through the Fathers*, Sobornost 7/7/78. I am indebted to this article in discussing the contemplative approach to Scripture.
31. Amedee Hallier, 'Sacred Scripture and the Fathers in the Monastic Theology of Aelred of Rievaulx', in *The Monastic Theology* of Aelred of Rievaulx, pp. 86ff.
32. George Moloney, *The Breath of the Mystic*, (Dimension Books 1974), p. 38.

6

Finding Community in Solitude

Not an Escape from Reality

In the first Eric Symes Abbot Memorial Lecture, Cardinal Hume said:

> The spiritual life is not an escape from reality but a journey into it. Our century, so deeply scarred by war, violence, deprivation and suffering, has been a time when many false gods have been toppled, and many misleading ideologies exposed. As we near the end of the second millennium people in Western Europe tend to be exhausted and confused but there are, I believe, undoubted signs that in and through pain and death we are discovering the beginnings of new life. The innate restlessness of the human spirit, the unexpected ways in which God manifests himself to us, all these could, and indeed should, lead us into a rediscovery of genuine spirituality. It is a task of much urgency.[1]

Only by responding to reality will genuine spirituality emerge, but never when it becomes an escape route into a haven of unreality, because it then becomes a *dead pietism*. This can happen in two ways which are not unrelated. First, for the individual, when it degenerates into an introverted cultivation of one's own soul, and secondly when it degenerates into a mere world-denying asceticism in which to escape from the vicissitudes and difficulties of life in the world. Then religion can become an opium by which to escape or be anaesthetized from one's alienated self, God and the world.

On the personal level, such dangers stem from getting

'hung-up' on the 'holy particularity of the soul and its needs', which so many books on prayer do foster. This was Thomas Merton's complaint. The priest, in helping his people to grow in prayer, needs to avoid this kind of hang-up if he is to avoid fostering an unreal and bogus spirituality. However he will only do this if he has travelled the road himself, and has discovered the essence of prayer in the smoking out of his own bogus interiority, by letting God smash the self-constructed idols of a God that will not disturb. This deeper exploration of reality which is the essence of prayer must lead into a deeper exploration of the real self and the letting-go of the false self that exists only in the imagination.

Thomas Merton elaborates on this when he writes about awareness, not only in relation to God but also in relation to self. In an unpublished manuscript Merton wrote:

> The first thing you have to do, before you start thinking about such a thing as contemplation, is to try to recover your basic natural unity, to reintegrate your compartmentalized being into a coordinated and simple whole, and learn to live as a unified human person. This means that you have to bring back the fragments of your distracted existence so that when you say 'I' there is really someone present to support the pronoun you have uttered.[2]

It is a matter of knowing who we are, which means, 'Before we can realize who we really are, we must become conscious of the fact that the person we think we are, here and now, is at best an imposter and a stranger'.[3] For this to happen, and it cannot be programmed through one's own ingenuity, there must be the renunciation of the limited and selfish self and an entrance into a new kind of existence where the false self is stripped away in authentic prayer. It is God working within us who interiorly transforms us into a new person so that we can act according to the Spirit given us by Him; the Spirit of our new life, the Spirit of Christ.[4]

Such an awareness leads to a true evaluation of self in the context of life as it is experienced. It is a kind of dying and rising experience where all illusion about self, God, and the world is unmasked, and where the heart is made pure, and the doors of perception opened. Only thus then can religion avoid becoming an opium by which to escape, because only thus can spirituality be something lived, rather than a mere adjustment to certain exterior norms of conduct which enable the individual to play an approved religious role.

Nor an Escape from the World

In this kind of vision our social concern as priests will grow, as we realize that our spirituality cannot ever degenerate into a world-denying asceticism in which to escape from the problems of life in the world. It will be from within the solitude of a contemplative spirituality that we shall come to a clearer vision of the world; humankind and nature in all their problematic actuality. The goal of Christian spirituality has been defined by God's intention for the whole of creation, so that it must embrace every aspect of man's life within the created world. Lorna Kendall, after describing the world as the object of God's love, in that He sent His Son into the world to save it, goes on to point out that:

> '... there is a proper sense in which Christians must be world-accepting as well as world-denying.... Moreover the contemplative sees the world which Jesus came to live in, to die for and to save, as much more than a geographical entity. He perceives it as a metaphysical reality, and he sees the responsibility of the Church to the world as including all that is normally meant by the phrase which describes the Church's function as being 'the servant of the world'. But the contemplative sees far more. His sense of responsibility, of 'mission' if you like, to the world involves a quality of openness to it, which enables him to find the living Christ in all human history and all human experience.[5]

Hence, our most important discovery will be the discovery of our fellow human beings in the depths of our solitude and prayer. Here we shall find ourselves present to them with the compassion of Christ. In the experience of a new solidarity with them, we will discover that we only discover the basis of community where we are most alone with God. No spirituality that is truly living can lead to God alone, but only to God together with all humankind.

This is not to advocate an activist and secular Christianity as expounded in recent times, though it does mean opening one's eyes to certain truths with which this kind of thinking was concerned—the need for an organic relationship between the sanctuary and the market-place. The basic intuition of Baron Von Hugel was his vision of the organic quality of all reality. His religion was not pietism.

> However much a man may be supremely and finally a religious animal, he is not only that; but he is physical and sexual, a fighting and artistic, a domestic and social, a political and philosophical animal as well.[6]

Von Hugel sees spirituality 'as concerning this total man in his stance before and as partner of the total real, both finite and infinite, both sacred and secular, both historical and eternal.'[7] This enables him to see spirituality as resolving dualisms; worldliness and monasticism, paschal cross and joy. At the same time he can see the point of, and be sympathetic to, the reactionary secularism of the Renaissance and the French Revolution, because they were reminding man that he had lost a sufficient interest in this wonderful world. So he can praise the 'world-seeking movement of his own time,' those who were striving for the social betterment of others and the good things of this life, within the limitations which only a spirit of unselfishness and a concern for God would reveal.

Such a spirituality embracing every aspect of man's life in this world evolves naturally out of belief in the Incarnation, which explains the true nature of all reality and all experience. What God is doing all the time. Within one's vision, born of an eschatological experience, the priest will see the world and understand it from the point of view of having been redeemed in Christ. A living, Christian spirituality will surely be aware of the victory of Christ and the reality of His Kingdom in the world even now, in all the confusion and chaos and risk, which is in evidence at the end of this second millennium. A priest's response to the world will not be in the form of losing his own special perspective, but in contributing a perspective which is not of this world, and which is liberated from the servitudes of the world in the negative and sterile sense. By virtue of this fact, a priest and his people will be enabled to be more truly present to the contemporary world by love, understanding, joy, peace, freedom, tolerance, and by a deep and Christ-like hope.

The Christian life-style which will emerge will have at its heart a spirituality which contains a sympathetic understanding of the world's legitimate aims, such as peace, individual freedom, justice and the sharing of resources in a world community. It will see these aspirations as the concern of everyone, but also be aware of what Voillaume calls *man in all his dimensions*, and so be able to see the obstacles frustrating contemporary man in his attainment of them. This must not lead to a rejection of contemporary secular man, because his struggle towards such aspirations appear to lack any concern for God. Rather must priests and Christians take seriously the valid effort of secular man to aspire to such values, which, good in themselves, doubtless come from God.

Cardinal Hume quotes Pope Paul VI, who appealed for evangelisers to speak to the world of a God whom the evangelists themselves should know and be familiar with as if they could 'see the invisible'. This requires stillness, attention, openness, love and communion. He was addressing a symposium of European Bishops in October 1985 and spoke of the qualities required in a herald of the Gospel. He said:

> We need heralds of the Gospel who are experts in humanity, who know the depths of the human heart, who can share the joys and hopes, the agonies and distress of people today but who are at the same time contemplatives who have fallen in

love with God.... [Such evangelists] must know, too, the
depths of the human heart—that heart when it rejoices,
admires or loves; that heart in its agonies, when it experiences
suffering, failure, emptiness. An ancient message can still
speak to a modern mind and warm today's hearts. The Gospel
is relevant, and is so in every age.[8]

Three Contemporary Figures

In our own generation there are three people in whom a
priest may find inspiration in this way of contemplative
living, Thomas Merton, Roger Schutz, and Rene Voillaume.
It is because Merton has wrestled with some of these issues
that Kenneth Leech sees him as being significant for the
Christian future: 'How to unite contemplation and action, the
"mystical" and the "prophetic", the revolution of the spirit
and political revolution.'[9] For Leech, these were going to be
the key issues of contemporary Christianity as they were the
key issues of Merton's spiritual quest. For Merton, mysticism and the social gospel stand together in an era in which
the most urgent search would be for the unity of the political
and the mystical, for the spiritual roots of liberation. His
contemplative experience had taught him that, to be a
Christian, it was impossible automatically to reject the world
or hold the world in contempt. The beginnings of this
discovery begin to emerge in *The Sign of Jonas*, where, after
ten years of solitude he reflects that it can never lead to God
alone, but only to God who is together with all humankind.
It is the diary of a man still on the way to discovering
solitude. A second, *Conjectures of a Guilty Bystander*, is of
a man, who having found his own solitude can engage
critically with his world. The source of his social and
political critique is not based on public debate and public
analysis, but rather on a contemplative penetration into the
heart of God.

Here is his point of departure, the place at which he
discovered the concrete man living on earth today. Through
his contemplative awareness and insight he was able to

expose the illusion and phoneyness of much in the social order and see the way forward to a restoration of right order and peace in the world.

> For Merton as for Ghandhi, non-violence was essentially a question of spirituality. Only the pure in heart can practise it. So politics and peace are inseparable from prayer, for it is in prayer that the heart is made pure. In his deep penetration into the passion of Christ in prayer, Merton became more sensitive to the world's evil, and more hungry for shalom... the search for spirituality and inner peace leading to a social theology which takes in the concern for peace, justice, and the freedom of man.[10]

This is what prompts Robert Voigt to describe Merton as this *Different Drummer*. Taking the idea from Thoreau who describes such a man as one who does not keep pace with his companions, perhaps because he hears a different drummer, Voigt uses it to describe the other side of Merton from the peace and quiet of the trappist monastery—the side which wrote of War and Racism, as twin scourges of twentieth century peace. For it was Merton's conviction that a person may not enter solitude to be away from the world, to shut himself off so that he can bask in the warmth of his own eclectic thoughts. Rather should it lead a person to become a better member of the community, whether of Church or State. Solitude is not, says Merton, 'a vocation to the warm narcissistic dream of a private religion. It is a vocation to become more fully awake.'[11] So a priest may well take note that this contemplative way of prayer has social implications. It means getting to know oneself in solitude before being able to influence others in multitude. The man who wants to be most effective in society limits his activity and needs solitude, where he can reflect upon God and thereby become a genuine lover of his fellow-man. This chimes in with what has already been quoted from Gregory the Great.

René Voillaume, Prior General of the Little Brothers of Jesus, and Roger Schutz, Prior of Taizé, are two other important modern figures. Both strike a contemporary note in their identification with the world as it is, and their emphasis on the need for greater rather than lesser engagement with the world. Yet for them this engagement must spring out of a life which has at its heart the practice of contemplative prayer. There is an insistent emphasis on its prime importance in the midst of worldly activity. At the same time they point out the futility of separating the contemplative from the active life. While both see contemplation to be the most intense form of prayer, what each is attempting to do is to live and practise the life of contemplation in a new way. This is not the completely enclosed condition traditional to this type of vocation. In fact, in this sense both men have been influenced by Charles de Foucauld, with whose initiative the contemplative life evolved into a life that could be lived in the world outside the traditional framework of the cloister.

Contemplative prayer is seen to be the channel of communication with God, the source of their life and inspiration. Equally, they see the need for their prayer to be, in itself, an effective instrument for the world. As a single, not a double vocation, they are seeking to express in their lives the harmony that must exist between contemplation and action, which every true contemplative has always recognized. The organization of their lives as individuals in community is an attempt to orientate this towards the world. The aim is not to convert the atheistic or unbelieving world in the accepted sense, but to emphasize that the Christian's duty in the world is to accept each person as he is, and then to offer him everything he wants in the way of love, care and affection.

The interesting fact about these three men is that they see the contemplative dimension of life—by reason of the spirituality which inspires it, the manner in which it is lived, and the means it employs—as being within the reach of all Christians. They are not chasing after the illusion of a *modern spirituality,* but as they penetrate more deeply into the *Christian Mystical Tradition* and allow it to come alive in themselves, they are able to live in time in the light of eternity, which recapitulates past, present, and future because everything is lived in contemporaneity with the reality of the Gospel.[12] Their concern therefore, is a wider diffusion of this contemplative way of living in the lives of Christians in their secular situation today.

Prayer and Availability

The context of spirituality for these three contemporary men of prayer is monastic, but the spirit and principle of such a way of prayerful living is adaptable to the world outside the cloister, where for most people an apostolic spirituality predominates. Here a framework of prayerful living has to be built into the daily round and common tasks of one's secular concerns so that they might be integrated into that prayer. For the priest the context in which he has to exercise his ministry is the place in which he is called to minister. As the monastery becomes for the monk his desert place in which he is called in order to empty himself of all selfish pursuits, so for the priest the context in which he lives out his ministry is for him a desert place, where he lives and meets with God who calls him to that same self-emptying. There in the spirit of his Lord and Master, he is called upon to experience the authentic self-emptying of our crucifixion. In a life of union with the Blessed Trinity, the priest is to live in prayerful solidarity with the people to whom God calls him to minister. Such a life can only make sense in the light of faith, whose sustenance is prayer, centred in the Word of God and the Eucharist. As priests we are called to a life of prayer in the world, to be at one and the same time united with Christ and with the world He came not to condemn but to save.

In many ways it is a misunderstood life, and the priest is a misunderstood man in a world that has marginalized him and made him seem irrelevant. There is also another sense in which he lives on the edge or margin of society. For it is only outside society that the desert place or *poustinia* where he meets with God can be found. There the priest goes to deepen fundamental human experience in the Kingdom which is not of this world, but in whose new life, values, and divine perspective lies the world's salvation. At the same time he is an irrelevant man, made so by the fact of death which for many makes life apparently absurd. Yet his life in being hidden with Christ in God, lives betwixt the two poles of Christian existence, Incarnation and Transfiguration. For in that union with Christ he joins in Jesus's own confrontation with the reality of death and resurrection, a particular death and resurrection that is situated in space and time, which unlike our own lives, is not limited by these things. What was peculiar to this death at a particular place and at a specific moment in history, was the devastating way in which it broke down the very barriers of death itself, so that all ages are affected by a radically new and creative act of God. The action of God in Incarnation, Death, Resurrection, and Transfiguration brings divinity into humanity and takes humanity into divinity.

By his participation in humanity, God has made it possible for man to participate in divinity, the mutual sharing and indwelling of God with humankind. In Christ's death is revealed the very secret of life, that to be truly and fully human man must share in the very life and nature of God, and the absence of such divine life in us is what makes us restless. Here the priest struggles with the fact of death in himself in order to find something deeper than death. The office of the priest as the marginal man—the man of the Eucharist, the man of prayer—is to go beyond death even in this life, to go beyond the dichotomy of life and death and in so doing to be a witness to life, *ars moriendi, ars vivendi.* This will not be easy in an Age that places so much emphasis on being relevant, on having an identity justified in terms of function. The pressures of an ethos that makes a priest irrelevant can be difficult to live in, and be destructive of priesthood itself, tempting the priest to justify his relevance in terms of that ethos. The mistake issues from viewing priesthood as an institution, reducing it to a structure, a function, a professional career-structure, rather than seeing it for what it is, a *charism,* a *vocation*, a manner of being. Its irrelevance has nothing to do with institutional structures but issues from the attitudes of a culture and Church in which the emphasis is predominantly pragmatic and almost totally orientated towards doing.

Are the chickens in the secularized theology of the sixties coming home to roost? Where is the life of holiness behind priestly ministry? Too much of what a priest does, or is seen and expected to be doing in the present climate of ecclesiastical life, become the terms in which a priest is defined, the managerial model which depersonalizes him and reduces him to the faceless administrator whose life has become a continual round of meetings. He is defined in terms of what is secondary to his life. What a priest is, must always be primary and determine what he does.

Praying the Parish

The term 'parish' is not used here in the literal sense but in a symbolical sense. It identifies the pastoral context of the priest's work, which may not be the geographical area in which he lives among the people to whom he ministers, but an educational establishment, hospital, institution, industrial or commercial complex. These are the different contexts for the priestly apostolate, but in all of them, the priest will be effective not by what he does, but by how he lives. For his life is lived at the heart of the Church in union with Christ in the life that he lives with the Father in the Holy Spirit. Rooted in that divine life, beyond all time and place, in the eschatological mystery, lies the reason, witness and meaning of the priest's life in today's secular world, which is unintelligible to a world that marginalizes that reality and the priest who finds his relevancy in it.

The timetabling of prayer will vary from one context to another, though the combinations of solitary and communal prayer will find their place. *Office* and *Eucharist*, affective and contemplative prayer, prayer without ceasing in the form of the Jesus Prayer, available to those to whom one ministers, all these elements should all find a place in the daily rhythm of each context. It will be a life of solitude and servanthood, the priest making himself available by being present among those to whom he is called to minister, but at the same time making space for silence and prayer. In his visiting of those people he comes as the *Theophoros* or God-bearer, the *Christophoros* or Christ-bearer, a living Eucharist of the divine presence, bringing a sympathetic ear and a compassionate heart in which they may find something of God's consolation, understanding and love. The priest brings more than mere professional help and professional skills, he brings the loving-kindness, goodness and friendship of God which is the only way in which he can bind up the broken-hearted and bring release to those who are captive in the variety of today's prisons.

At the same time it will be a life in which of necessity there will be spiritual warfare and suffering, that will be intensified for the priest because he will find his life and ministry living in close proximity to it. In solidarity with those who suffer he will share directly and indirectly the frustrations, anger, and incomprehensibility of that suffering, in what it does to those who suffer. The priest will share these struggles of his suffering people, the uncertainties such struggles bring, the sense of divine abandonment they induce, and the loneliness they cause. Only by solidarity and identification with his people can the priest share with them in the oppression of such acute suffering, a dimension of life which is not of this world. He must meet it in his own heart for that is part of his vocation, because it is only through his own interior warfare that he can learn the absolute necessity of total dependence upon God's love and providence. Here in the silence of his prayer where he dwells in the Blessed Trinity, he will meet the principalities and powers that challenge the redemptive power and love of God.

Identification Not Accommodation

It cannot be an easy and comfortable lifestyle, for it means a living engagement with the Cross at the heart of human life, but it is an engagement with the Cross in the knowledge and light of the Resurrection. As emphasized earlier, it is a way of living in which the way to life is through death; an existential disposing of ourselves in the way of the *Pascha Christi*, so that the death and resurrection of Christ can take hold of one's life and transform it. Only in this way can the priest bring that transfiguring heart in which the presence and light of Christ lives, the *Light of Light* which is the *Life* of men and which illuminates the world through us. It illuminates everything, enabling us to see that which distinguishes our Gospel in the light of the redemption a ruined world needs, and bringing a discernment that will enable the priest to see the difference between identification with a world in need of redemption, and accommodation to it. Such discernment, a perspective which is not of this world, will not come easily and we will most surely discover ourselves experiencing the dilemma of the apostles at the foot of the mount of Transfiguration, as their question, 'Why could not we cast him out?', becomes ours. The answer they received will be the answer we receive, 'Bring him to me', and as Michael Ramsey[13] comments, the only technique Christ mentions in rebuking the apostles is the 'science of the saints'. 'This kind goeth not out save by prayer and fasting'. It is this art and science of Christ and the apostles which has to be learned and practised and never taken for granted says Bishop Ramsey, but always to be painfully learnt.

In the great and crucial ages of the Church it has been this spirit of identification with the world, rather than accommodation to it, which saved the Church and her Word. This point is made by P.T. Forsyth at the beginning of the century.

[The Church] served a world she would not obey, in the name of a mastery it could neither confer nor withstand. She did not lead the world, nor echo it; she confronted it. If she borrowed the thought, the organization, the methods of the world, she did so voluntarily. And she only used them as a calculus. She was but requisitioning the ladders by which she escaped from the world, and rose to its command. She used the alloy not to debase the metal, but to make it workable, to make it a currency.[14]

In the first and greatest of its crises, the conflict with paganism, and especially gnosticism, he sees Athanasius rather than the Apologists as saving the Church for the future and for the Gospel. The line of the Apologists, the presentation of Christianity as the noblest of all the cultures, the most comprehensive of all the philosophies, the most efficient of all the ethics, the consummation of prophecies immanent in pagan humanity, and the apotheosis of all its latent powers, is a gnostic tendency, that is still present in contemporary gnosticism. It is the recrudescence in our own time of the old gnosis which makes the times so critical in its plausible antagonism to the Gospel. Athanasius developed everything that distinguished his position out of the principle of the experienced redemption of a ruined world. To achieve this he had to emulate St Paul and capture and transform the speculation of his day, 'converting the past rather than developing it', descending on the world rather than rising from it.

> He made the Church victorious by making it unpopular. He compelled the world to accommodate itself to him by preserving an evangelical isolation from it. He overcame the religious liberalism of his day by thought too profound to be welcome to the lazy public, and too positive to be welcome to the amateur discursive schools.

Forsyth believes that the Church has never, since the time of Athanasius, been in a position with the world so crucial as it is in this century:

> ... apostles of that Word are found speaking rather as adventurers of the soul. They are more drawn to the gnosis of

speculation, the occultism of science, the romance of the heart, the mysticism of imagination, than to the historic and ethical spirituality of the evangelical Christ the crucified. Now there will be no doubt of your popularity if you take that gnostic course with due eloquence, taste and confidence. For it expresses the formless longings and dim cravings of the subjectivity of the day. But it has not the future, because it misses the genuine note of the Gospel, and the objective Word and deed in the true moral crisis of the Soul. You will add religion to the vivid interests of the public; but you will not come with that authority which men at once resent and crave.[15]

In an educated Europe where the bulk of people either belong to no Church or are indifferent to the Church to which they belong, and where the culture is with the world rather than with the Gospel, the Church finds itself in the most critical time since the first centuries. As already noted there is much that can be learned from the Fathers that is relevant to the Church of today. Forsyth himself sees this relevance in adopting their stance in the main policy of the Church. While admitting that there will be accommodations to modern knowledge and modern criticism, he claims that amid all these adjustments to the world of natural and rational culture, the Church must in principle be detached.

With all her liberalism she must be positive. She must insist on the autonomy of faith in the matter of knowledge and certainty. She must descend on the world out of heaven from God. Her note is the supernatural note which distinguishes incarnation from immanence, redemption from evolution, the Kingdom of God from mere spiritual process. She must never be opportunist at the cost of being evangelical, liberal at the cost of being positive, too broad for the Cross's narrow way. And she must produce that impression on the whole, that impression of detachment from the world and of descent on it.... The Saviour of the world was not made or moulded by the world; and the world knew, and still knows in Him a presence that must be either obeyed or destroyed. He always looked down on the world He had to save. he always viewed it from God's side, and in God's interest. He always stood for God against the men he would save.[16]

But it was with pity he looked down, not with blame.

The priest comes in this same spirit, not as an obscurantist, but wearing the intelligible forms of living faith, divine but positive, ministering in Word and Sacrament that which is Humanity's hope and salvation, the divine energy in which he lives with Christ in the Father through the Holy Spirit, identified but not accommodated to the world Christ seeks to save.

Notes

1.   Cardinal Hume, *The Eric Symes Abbot Memorial Lecture No. 1*, (King's College London 1986).
2.   Thomas Merton, *The Inner Experience*, Notes on Contemplation (i), (ed. Patrick Hart), p. 3, which appeared in Cistercian Studies in 1983.
3.   Thomas Merton, *New Seeds of Contemplation* (Burns Oates 1962), p. 33.
4.   Thomas Merton, *Life and Holiness*, p. 57.
5.   Lorna Kendall, *Contemplative Living in the Contemporary World* (Mirfield Publications), p. 6.
6.   F.Von Hugel, *Essays and Addresses* I (Dent 1949), pp. 22–23.
7.   J.P. Whelan, *The Spirituality of Friedrich Von Hugel* (Collins 1971), p. 3.
8.   Cardinal Hume, *ibid.*, p. 6.
9.   K. Leech, 'Thomas Merton and the Present Spiritual Climate', *The Kingsman*, Journal of King's College London Faculty of Theology, No. 17, 1974–75, p. 43.
10.   Leech, *ibid.*, p. 45.
11.   Robert J.Voigt, *Thomas Merton: A Different Drummer,* (Liguori Publications 1972) pp. 95–96.
12.   This point was made in Chapter 2, on page 30.
13.   Michael Ramsey, *Canterbury Essays and Addresses* (SPCK 1964), p. 195.
14.   P.T. Forsyth, *Positive Preaching and the Modern Mind* (Independent Press 1960), p. 79.
15.   *Ibid.*, pp. 80–81.
16.   *Ibid.*, pp. 82–83.

7

Living Doctrine

A Time of Crisis

Just as Forsyth believes the Church to be in its most critical time since the first centuries, so too does Alexander Schmemann, who makes the point in his book of essays, *Church, World, Mission*. In the first essay of the book, *The Underlying Question*,[1] he offers an analysis of the crisis. The point he makes is that Western society has lost the organic relationship, and mutual integration that it once had with the Church so that its culture and way of life is no longer nurtured by the Church. Until more recent times this was the only way in which the Church related to the world, but today we find ourselves confronted with a *secularism* that is diametrically opposed to the spiritual nature and vocation of man. Its purpose is to challenge the Church in her essence and being, and to reduce her to values and philosophies of life which are not only different but often diametrically opposed to her vision and experience of God, Man, and life. Hence, the alienation of our culture from Christian values.

It is not so much the crisis itself that constitutes the problem, but the absence of any awareness that there is such a crisis. When Gareth Bennett in his *Crockford Preface*[2] raised this as a matter of profound significance in relation to the present state of Anglican theology, he was dismissed with the rhetoric of an unshakeable optimism and amazing self-righteousness, an official language whose purpose seemed to be to prevent the questions being raised and to stop doubts being expressed about the state of the Church.

Not only was there an unwillingness to read his meaning, but also it seemed, an incapacity. In the Church of England it was 'business as usual' in the spirit that wants to accommodate the Church to the culture's mode of understanding and acceptance, and hence, ways of doing things. Only then will the Church make inroads into secular culture, which will succumb and be reconverted to Christian life and manners. Reality is then clouded with pseudo-reality, as an unconscious surrender of the Christian consciousness to the secular world-view and way of life progresses.

The fundamental question not being asked is why the Christian Church should find itself under such threat, alienated from a society in which the secularist, materialistic mentality has triumphed. Instead it has turned its energies into conceiving a method of accommodating Christianity to anonymous modern man, to this man's mode of understanding which is essentially secularised and unchristian. This has resulted in the building of a system of beliefs on a non-Christian humanist foundation. In consequence, there has emerged in the social and religious life of our time, not only a false estimation of human nature and the practical banishment of the other-worldly element, but also a denial of the uniqueness of Christianity and the secularization of life and religion. For Anglicans this has meant that our heritage, the only heritage worth being preserved and lived by, the vision of God, Man, and life revealed in apostolic and catholic faith, is diluted and limited to a few superficial 'symbols'. Not only is 'secular' life, but also the Church's life progressively surrendered to that great western heresy, namely *secularism*, disorientating her whole approach to faith and order, parish life, liturgy, pastoral mission and education.

Schmemann has some interesting insights into this problem and the kind of treatment theology should provide. For those who claim identity and continuity with antiquity as the foundation of their faith and order, the problem of the past can never be a mere historical one. Of necessity it implies theology, '... because it is precisely for theology that the past presents itself—and not only today but always—as a *problem.*'[3] For Anglicans the past is of importance because it is the essential channel and carrier of Tradition, of the continuity of the Church in history, establishing her catholicity, that reveals her always as the same Church, the same faith, the same life. However, Tradition and past are not identical, and because the former comes from the latter, a true understanding of the past is impossible without obedience to the Tradition. Two dangers are to be avoided. First, a simple reduction of Tradition to the past identifying one with the other leads to the error of allowing the past to become the content as well as the criterion of Tradition. Secondly, the error of artificially separating Tradition from the past by means of their common evaluation in the present, which makes into tradition, only that which is arbitrarily considered to be acceptable, valid, and relevant. The task of theology maintains Schmemann is to seek ways of avoiding these dangers by making possible a correct *reading* of the Tradition, and therefore the proper understanding by the Church of her own past. This is not to deny that expressions of faith and life can and must change as the Church moves through history. Nevertheless, such change would need to be merely formal and not substantial and this conflicts with the liberalism that has captivated contemporary western theology. Its obsession with novelty and with being up-to-date as an expressive mark of superiority, breeds an unwillingness to come to terms with the past. In a theological method that integrates Scripture and Tradition, the secular and the contemporary, one finds Scripture and Tradition so subordinated to the secular and contemporary that they are often denied. A distinction is made between inductive (credal) and deductive (liberal or liberational) approaches, and a claim that the former should be replaced by the latter, as the captivity of a Protestant scholasticism tightens its grip. Consequently, Tradition has to pass the test of relevance in every context. This amounts to testing what is normatively Christian by the norms of a contemporary and secular culture.

Theology in Retreat

Such a climate has affected Anglicanism in a more fundamental way, for it has bred within our Anglican consciousness
an inability to come to terms with the past, due to the
confusion which exists about the true meaning and content
of our heritage and so of the Tradition. In consequence
there is an all too easy acceptance of the contemporary
world surrounding the Church; a world which challenges
her, and which reduces her life to a nominalism. This
becomes an obstacle preventing her from fulfilling her
essential mission of judging, evaluating, changing and
transforming the whole life of humankind. Gareth Bennett,
in *A Theology in Retreat*, pinpointed the crisis within
Anglicanism as being fundamentally theological.

> ... the most significant change is the decline of a distinctive
> Anglican theological method. In a magisterial study of the
> great divines of the seventeenth century, H.R. McAdoo[4]
> identified this as giving attention to Scripture, Tradition and
> Reason to establish doctrine. The context of such theological
> study was the corporate life of the Church and the end was to
> deepen its spirituality and forward its mission. Such a view of
> theology appears in official Anglican reports and in archiepis-
> copal addresses. But the last real exponent of classical Angli-
> can divinity was Archbishop Michael Ramsey whose many
> scholarly studies represent a last stand before the citadel fell
> to the repeated assaults of a younger generation of academics.
> The essential characteristic of the new theologians lies in their
> unease in combining the role of theologian and churchman,
> and their wish to study both Scripture and the patristic age
> without reference to the apologetic patterns of later
> Christianity.... Such a distancing of the modern Church from
> what had been regarded as its prescriptive sources clearly has
> serious consequences for Anglican ecclesiology, and this has
> been helpfully set out in Mr J.L. Houlden's book *Connections*
> (1986). Here he quite specifically rejects the notion of 'living
> in a tradition'. It would seem that modern man must live amid
> the ruins of past doctrinal and ecclesiastical systems, looking
> to the Scriptures only for themes and apprehensions which
> may inform his individual exploration of the mystery of God.[5]

Such a mind has imposed upon Anglicanism intellectual categories and thought-forms alien to the Anglican Tradition, emanating from a Protestant scholasticism whose integrating principle is justification by faith rather than the Incarnation.

It is not surprising to find this kind of theology isolated from the Church, the exclusive preserve of *a theology for academic theologians*, and therefore having little impact on her life. It represents an inner alienation from the sources, from the entire ethos of the patristic tradition of Anglicanism. It is nothing less and nothing more than a betrayal of her very life. In consequence, theology becomes divorced from life due to her failure to reveal the true saving and transforming power of the genuine Anglican Tradition. It is this tradition which has the power to make an effective and consistent critique of our present situation, and to offer an answer to the values, world-view and way of life which stem from today's intellectual and spiritual crisis. Schmemann would say that such theology fails because in a very subtle and unconscious way it remains conditioned by a double reduction. First, the reduction of theology to the historical, limiting its sources to texts and conceptual evidence and excluding the living experience of the Church, from which patristic theology stems, and to which it refers and bears testimony, and outside of which it cannot be understood in its total and precisely existential meaning and significance.[6] The same applies to classical Anglican divinity, for just as the theology of Athanasius cannot be understood apart from the liturgy of Bishop Serapion, so the theology of the Reformers and Carolines must find its origin and explanation in the Book of Common Prayer.

> Every living theology springs out of, and reflects, the worship of the Church.... When the theology of the Church is isolated from the Church's worship, it must always be misunderstood.[7]

The second reduction is intellectual, and consists in the reduction of the Tradition to a body of intellectual knowledge that deals with the Fathers, patristic or Anglican, as if they were thinkers working in concepts and ideas to build a self-contained and self-explanatory system. Such people are then transformed into authorities to be quoted to buttress and justify other ideas and affirmations, whose roots and ideology may have little to do with Anglican Faith and practice, so that what emerges is a western scholastic type of theology.

In the aftermath of the sixties and the played-out secular Christianity and social Gospel movements, an obsessive, but often insular and individualistic interest in spirituality has emerged, and the mystical has given birth to an atmosphere of religiosity. The priest of yesterday in the garb of psychotherapist becomes the staretz of today, but the essence of the act has not changed, for as Schmemann points out, at the heart of the religious epiphenomena of secularism is an individualism, a narcissism, which is expressive of a dominant *anthropocentrism*. He goes on to say that this situation will last as long as our theology does not overcome its own historical and intellectual reduction, and recover its pastoral, soteriological dimension and motivation. This soteriological motivation of theology is what prevents the *consensus patrum* from ever becoming a period piece, making it an eternal model of all true theology:

> ... its constant preoccupation with Truth as saving and trans-
> forming Truth, with truth as a matter of life and death and
> therefore its awareness of error as a truly demonic lie which
> distorts and mutilates life itself, leading man to spiritual
> suicide, literally to hell.[8]

This patristic existentialism, quite different from its contemporary philosophical expression, sees Christianity not primarily as an idea or a doctrine, but above all as an experience, the totally unique and *sui generis* experience of the Church, an experience which cannot be reduced to the categories of subjective and objective, individual and corporate.

Theology's Source and Datum

This experience has nothing to do with individual, subjective experience, or the religious experience of the individual. It is defined as the experience of the Church as *New Reality, New Creation, New Life*, not in terms of something detached and transcendent, some other world, but in terms of creation and life renewed and transformed in Christ, made into the knowledge of and communion with God and His eternal Kingdom. At the same time this experience is something radically new, because it is not of this world, but its gift and presence, continuity and fulfilment in this world is the Church. For the Fathers this *sui generis* experience of the Church, is what constitutes the self-evident source of theology. Not only is it the source, it is also the end to which theology bears witness, whose reality, saving and transforming power it proclaims, announces, reveals and defends. It is this dimension in the theology of the Fathers that makes it truly significant and without which they cannot be heard. Removing it reduces them to extrinsic formal authorities or ideas for discussion.

Bulgakov writes:

> The Church of Christ is not an institution; it is a new life with Christ and in Christ, guided by the Holy Spirit. Christ the Son of God, came to earth, was made man, uniting his divine life with that of humanity.[9]

In the words of Florovsky:

> ... the aim of its missionary activity is not merely to convey to people certain convictions or ideas, not even to impose on them a definite discipline or rule of life, but first of all to introduce them into the New Reality, to convert them, to bring them through by their faith and repentance to Christ Himself, that they should be born anew in Him and into Him by water and the Spirit. Thus the ministry of the Word is completed in the ministry of the Sacraments.[10]

Thomas Hopko defines the Church in terms of this same *sui generis* experience.

> [The Church] is the experience, here and now in this age, in time and in space, of the Kingdom of God not of this world, the new heaven and the new earth of the new man in the new

Jerusalem foretold by the prophets, fulfilled in the Messiah and His Spirit, and beheld in the mystic vision of the Apocalypse as the very life of the world to come. And she is not only total newness; she is total fullness as well: the participation in the humanity of Jesus, the incarnate Word, in whom dwells the whole 'fullness of deity bodily' and in whom human beings come to the 'fullness of life' (*Col. 2:9*). For 'of his fullness have we all received, grace upon grace' (*John 1:16*). She is the Church which is Christ's body and His bride, 'the fullness of Him who fills all in all' (*Eph. 1:23*).

Hopko goes on to say that there is an urgent need today for Christians to rediscover the Church. A critical need to go beyond all the rhetoric about theologies and traditions, beyond all claims about the contributions and enrichments of the many sects and denominations, and to discover again the reality of the 'household of God, which is the Church of the living God, the pillar and bulwark of the truth'.[11]

For the Fathers, the Church is always the subject of theology. The reality which makes it possible to know God and in Him, Man and the World, and the vehicle through which we learn the truth about all reality. It is only from within the experience of the Church that the World, by which is meant Man, Society, Nature and Life, can be truly known in its ultimate meaning and needs, and therefore be acted upon. But as Schmemann points out, this does not mean that they did not use the philosophy and cultural categories of the world in which they lived and of which they were an integral part. In fact, asserts Schmemann, they speak the language of their time, better and more consistently than we today speak the language of our time. But, when they use it, its meaning changes, its semantics are transformed as it becomes a tool of Christian thought and action, whereas modern theology succeeds at times in forcing even biblical and patristic language to carry ideas hopelessly alien, if not opposed to Christian faith and vision.[12] When the Church as experience of *New Life*, *New Reality*, is ignored and disregarded, it leads inevitably to the alienation of theology from the real life of the Church and by that token becomes useless to the world.

This *sui generis* experience of the Church is given in the Church's liturgy, the *lex orandi*, the Church's rule of prayer and worship which is the gift and expression of the Church's experience and which alone transcends the past, the present and the future. The Liturgy alone actualizes Tradition into life, fullness and power, for it is the epiphany or manifestation of this experience of *New Life,* the sacrament of Christ's coming and presence. In no way does this imply a liturgical reduction of theology.

> Just as they do not theologize about the Church, the Fathers do not theologize about the liturgy. Liturgy as the life, as the 'sacrament' of the Church is not the 'object' but the source of their theology because it is the epiphany of the Truth, of that fullness from which the 'mouth speaks'. Rooted in the experience of the Church as heaven on earth, the theology of the Fathers is free from 'this world' and therefore capable of facing it, of 'discerning' and changing it. Divorced from that experience, today's theology appears to live in a permanent identity-crisis, always in search of its own foundations, presuppositions and methods, of its 'legitimacy,' and therefore with no effect be it in the Church or in the world.[13]

To put the theological mind into the heart of the Church as experience, is to make the faith of the Church its source and datum, bringing that mind into a living relationship with certain events and making it a constant participant in these events in all their saving, life-giving and transfiguring reality. There theology will discover what the world needs, and it will not be ideology or even mere religion, that kind of sentimental spirituality so prevalent today.

> What the world needs... is above all a new experience of the world itself, of life itself in its personal and social, cosmical and eschatological dimensions. Of this experience the Church in her Orthodox understanding and 'experience,' is the revelation, the gift and the source. This experience our theology must 'rediscover' at its own source, so as to become its witness, its language in the Church and in the world.[14]

For the word 'Orthodox', 'patristic' and 'catholic' are adequate substitutes.

This is in harmony with Newbigin who finds a clue in Augustine and makes a plea for a new starting point beyond the assumptions of the Enlightenment, 'which begins as an act of trust in divine grace as something simply given to be received in faith and gratitude'. For him contemporary western Christianity is so compromised in its advanced state of syncretism, and in its uncritical acceptance of many of the assumptions of its contemporary secular culture, that it has almost lost the power to address a radical challenge to modern western civilisation. This chimes in with the convictions of Forsyth whose concern is that the pastor of today should like Athanasius 'descend on the world out of heaven from God', for he comes with what Gregory the Great describes as that inward knowledge, the fruit of having seen the Invisible, in stillness, silence, openness, love and communion, bringing not ideology, but the living power and energy of God himself. It is to come as a God-bearer, in a living knowledge and constant partaking of the *eschaton,* the end, which is what relates us as the Church to the world, providing us with the only source of the victory that overcomes the world. *Bring him to me, bring the world to me,* is Christ's plea, *This kind goeth not out save by prayer and fasting.* By her very nature the Church belongs to the end, the ultimate reality of the Kingdom of God.

Vision and Renewal

The loss of this dimension of eschatology[15]—a consciousness of this living knowledge and constant partaking of the *eschaton*, the ultimate reality of the Kingdom of God, as that which constitutes the true nature of the Church and gives her the only victory that will overcome the world—weakens the Church's mission in relation to secularism. Theology is diminished, one might even be bold enough to say destroyed, when what should be a coefficient of the entire theological enterprise is excluded. For such a living knowledge and constant partaking of the *eschaton*, should be shaping and permeating the entire Christian Faith and be its dynamic inspiration and motivation. It is not a mere doctrine, but an experience of the Kingdom of God. A highly positive experience which is identified with the world but not accommodated to it, judging and evaluating everything in the world, and through which the world is seen and experienced in a certain way. The eschatological dimension of theology ensures that its ultimate content and term of reference is not the world but the Kingdom of God. This is not being anti-world. Rather it is being pro-Kingdom; the Kingdom which came in the Incarnate, Crucified and Resurrected Lord, and the outpoured Holy Spirit, but which also comes *Now*, and is present in the Church and is centred on the Church's self-fulfilment in the Eucharist on the Lord's Day. Hence, the Church must live in the tension between an identifying *Yes* to the world, but also an equally emphatic non-accommodating *No*.

Only by bringing the world to share such an eschatological experience will secular culture be freed from what Maritain described (quoted in chapter 2) as the defect of post-Renaissance humanism, its *anthropocentrism*. This is also what Forsyth identified as the defect in the theology of his time. That theology, claimed Forsyth, was an expression of humanity's *egocentrism* more than of God's revelation.[16] Maritain's meaning is that contemporary man is shut up in himself and separated from Nature, Grace and God. Such an understanding of Man amputates and diminishes the potential for more abundant life that Man has the capacity to know and experience. Locked in his self-constructed and finite prison, he lives a restricted life-style, denying himself the freedom to grow and reach towards the infinite. Such an understanding of Man is completely alien to the biblical view that describes him as created in the image and likeness of God, completely alien to the vision of Man that such an experience of the Kingdom of God brings. The implication is that each of us is created with a capacity to share in the life of God and this is what makes us truly human.

> Man's basic need and ultimate purpose, then, is to become
> like God, to become one with God, thus the final goal of
> human existence is participation 'in the fullness of the divine
> life'. 'To believe that man is made in God's image is to
> believe that man is created for communion with God, and that
> if he rejects this communion he ceases to be properly man' ...
> the process of moral and spiritual growth through which man
> may achieve union with God.... Fr Thomas Hopko defines...
> as 'an unending process of growth and development' in which
> man becomes 'through gracious communion with God in
> freedom, all that God is by nature in the superabundant
> fullness of His inexhaustible and infinite Trinitarian being and
> life'.[17]

This is also the point that was made in the previous
chapter: that the action of God in Incarnation, Death, Resurrection and Transfiguration brings divinity into humanity and
takes humanity into divinity. By participation in humanity
God has made it possible for man to participate in divinity,
the mutual sharing and indwelling of God with humankind.
In Christ's death is revealed the very secret of life: that to be
truly and fully human, man must share in the very life and
nature of God, and the absence of such divine life in us is
what makes us restless. John Meyendorf describes this as the
central theme, or intuition of Byzantine theology:

> ... that man's nature is not a static, 'closed', autonomous
> entity, but a dynamic reality, determined in its very existence
> by its relationship to God. This relationship is seen as a
> process of ascent and as communion—man, created in the
> image of God, is called to achieve freely a 'divine similitude';
> his relationship to God is both a giveness and a task, an
> immediate experience and an expectation of even greater
> vision to be accomplished in a free effort of love. The dyna-
> mism of Byzantine anthropology can easily be contrasted with
> the static categories of 'nature' and 'grace' which dominated
> the thought of post-Augustinian Western Christianity; it can
> prove itself to be an essential frame of reference in the
> contemporary search for a new understanding of man....

Whether one deals with Trinitarian or Christological dogma, or whether one examines ecclesiology and sacramental doctrine, the mainstream of Byzantine theology uncovers the same vision of man, called to 'know' God, to 'participate' in His life, to be 'saved', not simply through an extrinsic action of God's, or through the rational cognition of propositional truths, but by 'becoming God'. And this theosis of man is radically different in Byzantine theology from the Neoplatonic return to an impersonal One: it is a new expression of the neo-testamental life 'in Christ' and in the 'communion of the Holy Spirit'.[18]

This way of understanding man's nature formed a universal tradition among the early Fathers, and brings us back to Athanasius who in the fourth century expressed it by saying that God became man in order that man might become God. He was only reiterating what Irenaeus had said in the second century when he declared that 'The glory of God is a living man and the life of man is the vision of God,' While it was meant to be taken literally it did not imply that we become God by nature, but rather in the sense of the *Second Letter of Peter*, 'partakers of the divine nature'. 'We remain creatures' said Maximos the Confessor, 'while becoming God by grace.' Our assimilation is not to some kind of moral example outside ourselves, but to Christ, dynamically and ontologically living in us through grace. Grace is just that; not some objective and static gift given to us, but an encounter with the living Person whose life is in us. To live 'in Christ', means an organic union between Christ and the human person, which is the expressed intention of Our Lord's high-priestly prayer: 'May they all be one, as thou, Father art in me, and I in Thee, so also may they be one in us.'[19]

In Christ then, God and man become one. In so far as a human being is 'in Christ'—through faith and through full participation in the life of the Church—he is one with God, because Christ's humanity is one with God. And it is through the gracious work of the Holy Spirit that the Christian believer is brought into an ever-developing and ever-deepening communion with God. The deification of man is therefore, a process of moral and spiritual growth toward God the Father, through God the Son and in God the Holy Spirit. In this way, man may become a 'partaker of the divine nature' (2 *Peter 1:4*), a participant in the energies and eternal life of the triune God.[20]

Where the spirit of this doctrinal tradition has been allowed to return in a concrete and living way, it has led to impressive and life-giving renewal. Such was the inspiration for renewal in Aelred of Rievaulx and the great flowering of Cistercian life in the twelfth century. In the seventeenth century St Francis de Sales found in these early sources of spiritual doctrine, particularly in St John Chrysostom, the life-giving renewal that his own life needed. Through him acting as both Bishop and spiritual counsellor, God was to renew his Church.

Anglican Divinity

There have always been Anglican divines, parish priests as well as academics, who have not only been formed by the mind of the Fathers, but who have been ready to vindicate this same patristic doctrinal tradition as essential to Anglican divinity. The roots of this patristic orientation are traceable to the Anglican Reformers of the sixteenth century who were the first to make the appeal to the Fathers a foundation stone of their divinity, building their theology on patristic dogma and practice. This *appeal to antiquity*, as it came to be called, continued as part of the Anglican theological method, and always included as integral a concern for Church history and the 'proper', historical setting of the Bible, the living apostolic community, the catholic Church of the Fathers. Herein is ensured authoritatively, normatively and critically, the historic continuity of the apostolic community and her apostolic faith and praxis. This ecclesial dimension, the patristic and catholic ekkelsiastikon *phronema*, was appropriated by Anglicanism and made the basis of Christian living, the context of Christian thinking. Such ecclesiastical understanding, does not add anything to Scripture, but is the only means to ascertain and disclose fully the true meaning of Scripture. It was Fr George Tavard SJ who maintained that in making Scripture and Tradition a mutually inclusive and self-evident basis of Anglicanism, she maintains a consistency with the patristic spirit and makes her a better representative of the theology of the catholic eras, patristic and medieval, than many of the Catholic writers of the Counter-Reformation period.[21] This ecclesial context of Anglican divinity understands the Church as bearing witness to the truth not by reminiscence or from the words of others, but from its own living, unceasing experience, from its catholic fullness which has its roots in continuity with the Primitive Church. Therein consists that *tradition of truth* in which the apostolic teaching is not so much an unchangeable example to be repeated or imitated, as an eternally living and inexhaustible source of life and inspiration. Tradition is the constant abiding Spirit, not only the memory of words, and is therefore a charismatic not an historical principle. Together with Scripture it contains the truth of divine revelation, a truth that lives in the Church.

Within this tradition of Anglican divinity stand two representative figures, Richard Hooker and Lancelot Andrewes, whose work was seminal in establishing Anglican identity and in developing it on the patristic foundation laid by the Anglican Reformers of the sixteenth century. These Caroline divines went further than their reforming predecessors, whose interest in the Fathers was as a means to prove what had been primitive doctrine and practice, using the thought and piety of the Fathers within the structure of their own theological exposition. In the theology of these divines, thinking and praying are indissolubly connected, in an orthodoxy which was not a static repetition of the past but a living, growing pattern of truth. The fusion of thought and feeling in these theologians is what A.M. Allchin tells us drew that twentieth-century man of letters T.S. Eliot back to Christian faith and life and prompted his small book of essays *For Lancelot Andrewes*. For Eliot Andrewes embodied in himself, the theology and the devotion which marks the best men of this age.[22] For him, Hooker and Andrewes made the English Church more worthy of intellectual assent, and in them as in the actual life and worship of the period, he found a catholicism which was not ignorant either of the Renaissance or the Reformation, a tradition which had already moved into the modern world.

> It was a way of living and thinking the Christian tradition which had taken humanism and criticism into itself, without being destroyed by them....[23]

In them we find that same patristic vision of man, which like theirs is integrally related to, and organically connected with, their own understanding of Trinitarian and Christological dogma, ecclesiology and sacramental doctrine. Fr Lionel Thornton CR,[24] points out that for Hooker the grace of the sacraments is the last link in a series whose *terminus* is the participation of the saints in the life of God, after stating that Hooker does not shrink from using the Catholic phrase *deification of man,* and in doing so follows Irenaeus, Clement, Athanasius and the main current of Greek theology. Canon Allchin tells us that the key concepts in Hooker's theological thought are to be found 'in terms such as mutual participation and conjunction, co-inherence and perichoresis. God is in Christ; Christ is in us; we are in him'[25] For Hooker the archetype of participation is the mutual indwelling of the Father, Son and Holy Spirit in the oneness of the Blessed Trinity, in which there is a law of self-impartation alongside that mutual indwelling of divine life and love that exists between the Father and the Son.

> Life as all other gifts and benefits groweth originally from the Father, and cometh not to us but by the Son, (*1 John 5:11*) nor by the Son to any of us in particular but through the Spirit (*Romans 8:10*). For this cause the Apostle wisheth to the Church of Corinth 'The grace of our Lord Jesus Christ, the

love of God, and the fellowship of the Holy Ghost' (*2 Cor. 13:13*) which three St Peter comprehendeth in one, 'the participation of the divine nature' (*2 Peter 1:4*).

Hooker is concerned to point out that our coinherence in Christ is far more than a sharing of the same human nature.

> The Church is in Christ as Eve was in Adam. yea by grace we are every one of us in Christ and in his Church, as by nature we are in those first parents. God made Eve of the rib of Adam. And his Church he frameth out of the very flesh, the very wounded and bleeding side of the Son of Man. His body crucified and his blood shed for the life of the world, are the true elements of that heavenly being, which maketh us such as himself is of whom we come (*John 1:4–9*).[26]

Commenting on this, Canon Allchin writes:

> It is true that Hooker here avoids the explicit language of theosis, (or deification) but it does not escape our attention that when he speaks of Christ, making us such as himself is, he affirms the underlying mystery which the word expresses.[27]

On the divine and human sides of the Incarnation Our Lord uniquely participates in the Father by mutual indwelling, enabling all created things to participate in the life of God and in some degree enjoy mutual indwelling with him. The self-impartation which exists within the Godhead finds expression in a self-impartation of God to his creation, so that creation and redemption become two modes in which created beings participate in the life of God. In another context Allchin affirms Hooker's understanding of participation in terms of deification[28]. With the support of C.S. Lewis, whose theology was greatly influenced by Hooker, Canon Allchin quotes Lewis's words on Hooker in the *Oxford History of English Literature.*[29] Here Lewis speaks of Hooker's model universe as being drenched with deity and Hooker's words 'All things that are of God, have God in them and they in himself likewise, and yet their substance and his are very different.' Lewis spells out what this presence of the transcendent God in his world implies, keeping together all things that can easily be set in opposition.

> Reason as well as revelation, nature as well as grace, the commonwealth as well as the Church, are equally though diversely, 'of God'.... All kinds of knowledge, all good arts, sciences and disciplines... we meet in all levels the divine wisdom shining out through 'the beautiful variety of things' in 'their manifold and yet harmonious dissimilitude'.

This is nothing less than the patristic vision of God's creation filled with his energy and wisdom, the presence of God participating in his world, which can be the only context within which to speak of man's participation in God in terms of deification. 'The Word of God, who is God wills in all things and at all times to work the mystery of his embodiment.'[30] Within this context Hooker expounds a vision of man which finds its fulfilment in God; a theocentric humanism.

> If then in him we are blessed, it is by force of participation and conjunction with him... so that although we be men, yet being into God united we live as it were the life of God.[31]

The theme of deification emerges in Hooker's description of man's relationship to God in terms of conjunction and participation, terms with a technical significance which occur frequently in this context. Because man is made for God and can only find fulfilment in him, there is a restlessness and longing for self-transcendence:

> ... that which exceeds the reach of sense; yea somewhat above the capacity of reason, somewhat divine and heavenly, which with hidden exultation, he rather surmiseth than conceiveth....[32]

God's initiative in Christ leads man into the kingdom of heaven where life becomes a constant growth into the world of everlasting life.

Canon Allchin cites Olivier Loyer,[33] speaking of Hooker's vision of man as of a being inhabited by 'a natural desire for a supernatural end'. Loyer shows how for Hooker the

concept of participation becomes a key to be used to unlock
many different areas of theological thought:

> ... not only the economy of creation, but also the Trinitarian
> economy and the economy of salvation. In the heart of the
> Trinity, participation becomes procession of the persons, the
> circumcession, underlining at once their distinction and their
> mutual coinherence. At the level of redemption it expresses
> the mystery of our adoption....

God is in us, we are in him by way of a mutual participation, in which creature and Creator remain distinct while
being no longer separate.

> Following this line of thought and working within the termi-
> nology of the western scholastic tradition, Hooker opens up
> the way for a reaffirmation of the patristic conviction that man
> can indeed become a partaker of the divine nature, but only
> and always by gift and grace, never by right and nature.

The theological implications of this, Hooker spells out in his
doctrine of the Church and the Sacraments which he organically connects to his reaffirmation of the Chalcedonian
Christology.

This doctrine of *theosis* forms an essential and important
strand in the theology of Lancelot Andrewes, where it is the
natural consequence and completion of the doctrine of the
Incarnation. Canon Allchin discusses this in two of his
works, an essay, *Trinity and Incarnation in the Anglican
Tradition,*[34] and his book *Participation in God.*[35] In the
former he quotes from a sermon for Pentecost,[36] comparing
the work of Christ with the Holy Spirit. Here Andrewes
speaks of the mystery of his Incarnation and the mystery of
our inspiration as:

> ... great mysteries of godliness [in both, God being] mani-
> fested in the flesh... in the former by the union of his Son; in
> the latter by the communion of his blessed Spirit... without
> either of them we are not complete, we have not our accom-
> plishment; but by both of them we have, and that fully, even
> by this day's royal exchange. Whereby, as before he of ours,

so now we of his are made partakers. he clothed with our flesh, and we invested with his Spirit. The great promise of the Old Testament accomplished, that he should partake our human nature; and the great and precious promise of the New, that we should be *consortes divinae naturae*, 'partake of his divine nature', both are this day accomplished.

Here as Allchin remarks there is no reticence about the doctrine of *theosis* that is characteristic of other Western theologians.

Rather we find a renewal of the teaching of the Fathers in its fullness, a fullness which includes such themes as the constant progress into God described by Gregory of Nyssa.

Christian life is continuous growth, Gregory's idea of *epektesis*, of never having arrived, but of pressing on in pursuit of still purer, more vital experience of God's light and truth, where each fulfilment contains in itself the impulse to further growth.

... to be made partakers of the Spirit, is to be made partakers 'of the divine nature'.... Partakers of the Spirit we are, by receiving grace.... The state of grace is the perfection of this life, to grow still from grace to grace, to profit in it. As to go on still forward is the perfection of the traveller, to draw still nearer and nearer to his journey's end.[37]

In his second work, after establishing Andrewes' capacity to preach a coherent and organic theology, he cites T.S. Eliot's essay *For Lancelot Andrewes,* to ally with this 'a quality or depth in his writing'. Eliot speaks of Andrewes as being completely absorbed in his subject, his emotion growing the more deeply he penetrates the mystery he seeks to grasp. This emotion Eliot describes as contemplative, something evoked by the object of contemplation, wholly contained in and explained by its object. In Andrewes, Allchin points out, thinking and feeling have been fused together:

... a man of whom what is within, what is subjective, is wholly evoked by what is beyond, the object of his contem-plation, in whom subjective and objective are thus reconciled

and at one. A man... totally absorbed in his subject... which is
more than metaphorical... such a one should be able to speak
to us about participation in the divine nature, for he speaks
from experience.[38]

So Andrewes does speak, expounding the meaning of
Emmanuel, what *God with us* means, in a Christmas sermon
where he demonstrates a living integration linking the
doctrines of Incarnation, Adoption, deification, Virgin-Birth,
Baptismal birth, and the life-giving action of the Holy Spirit
in the womb and font. God is with us:

> ... to make us that to God that he was this day to man. And
> this indeed was the chief end of his being 'with us'; to give
> us a *posse fieri*, a capacity, 'a power to be made sons of God',
> by being born again of water and the Spirit; *Originem quam
> sumpsit ex utero Virginis posuit in fonte Baptismatis*, 'the
> same original that himself took in the womb of the virgin to
> usward the same hath he placed for us in the fountain of
> baptism to Godward,' well therefore called the womb of the
> Church *sustiochon* to the Virgin's womb, with a power given
> it of *concipiet et pariet filiosto* God. So his being conceived and
> born of the Son of man doth conceive and bring forth (*filiato,
> filiationem*) our being born, our being sons of God, his partici-
> pation of our human, our participation of his divine nature.[39]

In no way can Easter be separated from Christmas, nor
Resurrection from Incarnation nor the consequences of this
Christian mystery, any disjunction between the union of
human and divine. Christmas needs Easter, '... the still
greater mystery of death and resurrection, where we see the
divine-human interchange in a new and still more striking
perspective'[40] in a new birth from the dead. Here a quotation
compares and contrasts these two births in which Easter is
described as a second Christmas. Christmas unites Christ
with humankind, not in its sin but in its infirmities, mortality
and death and in a brotherhood which death dissolves. Easter
heralds a second birth from the grave.

> Before he was ours, now we are his. That was by the mother's
> side; so he ours. This is *patrem vestrum*, the father's side; so

we his. But half-brothers before, never the whole blood till
now. Now by the Father and mother both, *fratres germani,
fratres fraterrimi,* we can not be more.... This is the better day
by far.[41]

Any understanding of Andrewes' teaching on deification
cannot be fully understood without seeing its organic
connection with his pneumatology which Lossky says is
given significance by the stress he puts on the deification of
man as the supreme goal of salvation.

It is a matter of the union of man with God in Christ by the
Holy Spirit. If his theology is at once Christological and
Pneumatological, it is because, in his vision of salvation, he
has made profoundly his own the image of St Irenaeus
according to which the Son and the Spirit are 'the two hands'
of the Father. This image expresses the complementarity, the
reciprocity, the unity and the distinction of the two Persons in
the divine economy. At the same time, and above all, it shows
clearly that the divine economy is the action of the Three
Persons of the Holy Trinity. As we have seen, Andrewes
never forgets this.[42]

Andrewes' vision is Trinitarian, a pastoral theologian with
a theology to be preached, and therefore with a practical
purpose, nothing less than to participate in the divine life
Christ lives with the Father in the Holy Spirit. It is a life
within the Church, a sacramental life in worship and in
prayer, a life of continual movement and growth in the very
life of God himself. This is *saving life, salvation.* In this
work Christ and the Spirit cannot be separated.

The Holy Spirit reveals the divinity of the Son who is the
Image of the Father. (*2 Cor. 4:4*) The man who becomes a
'partaker of the divine nature' (*2 Pet. 1:4*) enters into communion with the common nature of the Three in so far as it is
manifested from the Father through the Son, in the Holy Spirit.
By the uncreated grace of the Holy Spirit, God, that is to say
the Trinity, comes to dwell in him, and man comes, one could
say, 'in the Holy Spirit through the Son, to the Father'.[43]

The Incarnation of God is for the breathing into man of the

very life of God, and this keeping together of Incarnation and Inspiration, *Incarnatio* and *Inspiratio*, God clothed in flesh and man invested with divinity, dominates Andrewes' sermons for Pentecost. Thereby are we caught up in the very life and being of the Trinity.

Such Anglican divinity illustrates that the following of the Fathers, the *appeal to antiquity*, is not a reference to abstract tradition, to formulas and propositions, to form the content of repetition. Only when it suffers from such a double reduction, historical and intellectual, does it become culturally irrelevant. At the heart of Caroline theology was the conviction that Anglicanism was not merely a child of the Primitive Church, but that she is at one with her, she is and remains an essential part of that *Church of the Fathers*. Their following of the Fathers, was not the buttressing of their thinking with patristic quotations, but the acquiring of the patristic mind, in which they theologized *ad mentem Patrum,* which saved them from being determined by the fashions of the Puritanism and Calvinism of their day. For them the Fathers became, not mere relics of the past but living witnesses and real contemporaries, in which their authentically charismatic life in the Church is what constitutes their essential feature. In order to see more clearly this open-ended scope of the Patristic era, the basic principle of Gregory of Nazianzen concerning theology is particularly pertinent.

> If one is to accept his axiomatic definition of theologians as being 'those tried and advanced in theory (*i.e.* contemplative vision)... and above all, those purified or, at least undergoing purification' [*Oration I.3*], and if one believes that the supreme form of *theognosia* in Scripture is the vision of God's glory as beheld by Moses, then, one must acknowledge that the high points of theology are not confined to one specific 'golden' age but pervade every age which happens to be blessed with those 'advanced in theory' (*i.e.* vision)... and purified. By analogy, there is a decay in the theological world when such saints are wanting.[44]

This is precisely a following of the mind of the Fathers in

which one resists the influences of a secular determinism. The Fathers are more up to date than many of our contemporary theologians, for the reason that they were dealing with things and not with maps. They were concerned not so much with what man can believe, as with what God has done for man. In this present time of crisis we have to enlarge our perspective, acknowledge the masters of old, patristic and Caroline alike, and attempt for our own age an existential synthesis of Christian experience, the *sui generis* experience of the Church, centred in that central vision of Christian faith, Jesus Christ, God and Redeemer, Crucified, Risen, Transfigured and Glorified.

Man the Icon of God

Central to the foregoing is *Man as the Icon of God,* a consequence of the Incarnation which inspires the Church's prayer for the Sunday after Christmas in the *ASB.* Here we pray, '... grant that, as he came to share our humanity, so we may share the life of his divinity...' and which is diametrically opposed to the *anthropocentric* vision of man which is the essence of secularism. As an icon of God, man's full nature cannot be understood unless he is seen in relationship to the organic whole of which he forms a part. This implies that he must live within a particular framework of belief and worship, in order that he might manifest, convey and give support to the spiritual facts undergirding human existence and underlying the liturgical drama of the Eucharist. Here life is given a Eucharistic shape, that Man may participate in it and manifest it, and realize that just as the destiny of Jesus was bound up with that piece of Bread, so too is his. In this piece of Bread you will find your identity and destiny, nourished from *My Food,* which is to do the will of him who sent me. What happens in the Eucharist must happen in us if we are to be the Body of Christ and be a vehicle of the divine life—we must be taken, consecrated, broken and given.

What is communicated is a new experience of *Life,*

because such *Life* gives us the capacity to give visible shape to death, suffering, love, fear, and grief. It gives us the power to take these things into ourselves, to draw them back into *Life*, that they may be reshaped by *Life* itself. Life for Man is more than survival because the reality in which we live is the Resurrection, and the purpose of the Eucharist is to convey this experience of reality as the consummation of Incarnation and Transfiguration, the two poles of the Christian scheme of salvation. For as the Incarnation signifies the entry of Spirit into matter, into human and natural existence, and the Transfiguration signifies the consequence of this, the spiritualization of human and natural existence, the Eucharist recapitulates in the life of man this *saving life*. The Athanasian dictum, God became man, that man might become God, expresses this scheme of salvation, and the Eucharist becomes the vehicle of this divine life, continuing through time the redemptive activity of Christ, with the capacity to bring about man's salvation. Here, in the Eucharist, the world will find what Schmemann says it needs, a new experience of the world itself, of *life* itself, in its personal and social, cosmical and eschatological dimensions, and of which the Church is the revelation, the gift, and the source.

The nature of man as an icon of God has more to it than being a mere sign or indication of something else. By virtue of sharing in the nature of the object of which it is an image, there is an interpenetration of the one in the other, a physical fusion though not confusion. Hence knowing the image instantly makes one conscious of the object it reveals, effecting rather than merely indicating what it really signifies. Thereby, to the extent that one is open and receptive to its influence, one actually experiences the *life* which it mysteriously mirrors and enshrines. The Eucharist is such an image of divine life which is the light of men, and was made flesh and dwelt among us. To those who open themselves to this reality of divine life, receiving him and believing in his name, he will give power to become children of God, *born not of blood nor of the will of the flesh, nor of the will of*

man but of God (*John 1:12–13*). The Eucharist communi-
cates to Man this divine life, Man becoming in his turn a
centre of power, an incarnation of the spiritual energy of
God. He participates in, and partakes of, the *Life* that is more
than human, and thereby is able to induce in others a
consciousness of this more than human life which he
embodies. Eucharistic Man testifies to the basic realities of
the Christian Faith, to the reality of the divine penetration in
the human and natural world, and to the reality of sanctification which results from this.

As an icon, Eucharistic Man is not to be a mere imitation
or copy of humanist models of self-realization and self-
fulfilment. Rather must he convey a picture of the divine
world order, a picture of how things are in their true state,
how things are in the eyes of God and not as they appear to
us from our limited human angle of vision. Such vision is
only possible by living in the Spirit of God, for the likeness
of God in man is a spiritual likeness and exists only in the
Spirit, and this kind of knowledge only comes through
personal participation in the object of knowing, an inward
merging and identity with it. It is this *oneing with God,* to
use Julian's phrase, which widens one's vision, giving the
necessary capacity to be able to accept that which man is to
express, until it lives in him with its own inherent vitality.
His life becomes one of unceasing renewal and growth
through an interior disciplined living in the Spirit, in whom
are recreated the spiritual realities of which man is to be the
icon.

Understanding Man in this sense, not only gives us a
means of presenting doctrine in a living way, but also
enables its spiritual realization. For doctrine is not theory,
but realities in which we live, and through which we receive
the vision to see and know what *life* is. The essence of the
Christian Creed is not mere thought, but experience—the
experience and awareness of the grace, love, fellowship and
joy of 'God with us'. Living comes before thinking and
thought must never be confused with existence. Christian
thought is never the mere product of the mind and like life

it is larger than logic. So we must learn to worship before we can properly know how to inquire, and doxology is the best form in which to communicate doctrine. Therefore *Man as an icon of God* is to be a living illustration of the Christian Creed, presenting theology existentially as he integrates in his being a doctrine of Creation, Incarnation, Crucifixion, Resurrection and Transfiguration. He is to be a living image of the Christian scheme of salvation, instructing by illustration in the dogmatic truths of the Faith.

This Faith, being more than mere ideas ,becomes a way of growing in the Spirit which prevents such ideas from becoming static. Doctrine is living reality, states of power within man as well as within the universe and which as an icon man is to image. Being in communion with the life of what he images, man becomes such a centre of power in himself, an incarnation of the spiritual energy of God. Therefore he is able both to communicate to others, and to induce in them, a consciousness of this power and presence of divinity, in the language of a life that manifests an ever-increasing measure of discretion and discernment. Expressing in a lifestyle that which is rooted in a communion of life not his own. Man the icon, not only manifests the true purpose of man, but draws others by the power of the life in which he lives to a realization of that purpose. For it is a vision of wholeness that holds together in a single vision, eternity and time, spirit and matter, the divine and the human.

Notes

1.   Alexander Schmemann, 'The Underlying Question' in *Church, World, Mission* (SVS Press 1979).

2.   Gareth Bennett, *Preface to Crockford's Clerical Directory 1987–88.*

3.   Schmemann, *ibid.*, p. 14. I am indebted to Schmemann for some insights I have developed in my own way.

4.   H.R. McAdoo, *The Spirit of Anglicanism* (A. & C. Black 1965).

5.   Bennett, *ibid.*

6. Schmemann, *ibid.*
7. Nathanael Micklem, 'The History of Christian Doctrine' in *The Study of Theology* ed. K. Kirk (Hodder and Stoughton 1939), p. 291.
8. Schmemann, *ibid.*
9. S. Bulgakov, *The Orthodox Church* (SVS Press 1988), p. 1.
10. G. Florovsky, *Bible, Church,Tradition: An Eastern Orthodox Perspective* (Nordland 1972), p. 69.
11. T. Hopko, *All the Fullness of God* (SVS Press 1982), pp. 34–35.
12. Schmemann, *ibid.*
13. Schmemann, *ibid.*, p. 22.
14. *Schmemann, ibid.*, p. 22.
15. *Schmemann, ibid.*, ch. 1.
16. John H. Rodgers, *The Theology of P.T. Forsyth*, (Independent Press 1965), p. 17.
17. George Cronk, *The Message of the Bible, An Orthodox Christian Perspective*, (SVS Press, 1982), p. 36.
18. J. Meyendorf, *Byzantine Theology*, (Fordham University Press 1983), pp. 2–3.
19. *John 17:21.*
20. Cronk, *ibid.*, p. 37.
21. G. Tavard, *Holy Writ or Holy Church* (Burns Oates 1959), p. 245.
22. A.M. Allchin, *The Dynamic of Tradition* (DLT 1981), p. 56.
23. Allchin, *ibid.*, p. 57.
24. L. Thornton, *Richard Hooker* (SPCK 1924) pp. 71, 68.
25. A.M. Allchin, *The Kingdom of Love and Knowledge* (DLT 1979), p. 96.
26. Richard Hooker, *Laws of Ecclesiastical Polity*, V.lvi, 7.
27. Allchin, *ibid.* p. 97.
28. Allchin, *Participation in God* (DLT 1988), p. 8.
29. (Oxford 1954), p. 460.
30. Maximos the Confessor, cited by Allchin, *ibid.*, p. 9.
31. Hooker, *ibid.*, I.xi.2.
32. Hooker, *ibid.*, I.xi.4.
33. Olivier Loyer, *L'Anglicanisme de Richard Hooker,* (Paris 1979), vol I p. 353ff, cited by Allchin *ibid.*, p. 12ff.
34. Allchin, *The Kingdom of Love and Knowledge*, p. 98.
35. *Participation in God,* pp. 15–23.
36. Andrewes, *Works* (L.A.C.T.) pp. 108–9.
37. Cited by Allchin, *The Kingdom of Love and Knowledge*, p. 99.

38.   Allchin, *Participation in God*, p.16.
39.   Andrewes, *Works* (L.A.C.T.) Vol. I, 'Sermons' p. 150.
40.   Allchin, *ibid.*, p. 17.
41.   Andrewes, *Works* (L.A.C.T. 1841-54) Vol. I, p. 122; cited by
       Allchin pp. 17–18.
42.   N. Lossky, *Lancelot Andrewes the Preacher*, trans. A. Louth
       (Oxford 1991), pp. 334–335.
43.   Lossky, *ibid.* p. 335.
44.   John Chryssagis, 'The Age of the Fathers, a perennial pres-
       ence', *St Mark's Review*, Winter 1988, p. 31.

8

Eschol

An Agenda for the Church

Our concern is not merely the renewal of the priesthood, but ultimately the destiny of the Church, which no longer can claim integration with society. In the contemporary pastoral context we are faced with a *secularism* which is opposed to the true dignity and spiritual destiny of human beings. Man today is less fundamental in his thinking than he has ever been. The Christian mind, in general, is unaware of any conflict or crisis, and therefore it can no longer understand the world in which it seeks to witness to Christ. Rather does it seek to accommodate the Church to the methods and thought patterns of the world, in the desperate hope that it might in this way make some inroads. Let it be our concern in the face of this reductionist trend, to be motivated to seek a recovery of what Anglicans in their appeal to antiquity have understood by Tradition, as a living resource, a way of living and thinking in the Church-in-the-world.

Here in the larger room of the Christian centuries in which the Holy Catholic Church lives, we will find what will enrich, invigorate, give beauty, proportion, and force, to our theology. Our vision will have about it the catholicity, the widemindedness, the freshness, the suppleness and sanity of Christian antiquity, as we see the Christian faith as an integral whole with its natural centre in the Incarnation, the Church as an organism where dogma, prayer and life are one whole, and where, '... the issue is not only one of intellectual clarity but of a union of human lives with God in the way of holiness...'. Renewal in catholic truth will only come from a reconstruction of the *One Holy Catholic and Apostolic Church*, not through the construction of some external religious or cultural form, or ideology. It can come only, when the living pattern of catholic truth is embodied in people imbued with the life-giving power of God, who in Christ has taken our human nature, redeemed it and perfected it for ever. The *lex credendi*, tradition, catholic dogma and doctrine is not a backcloth of abstract theory to be adapted according to the fashions of the *Age*. This is the *reality* in which we live, *the union of human lives with God in the way of holiness*. Through it we see refracted the meaning of all human existence—the economies of creation and redemption. Hence the need to know this truth in the personal depth of our being, for it is the Christ of the apostles as the life-giving Spirit active in the history of humankind, leading it to conformity with his spiritual and perfect form. Here in the Mystery of Christ, present in the history of mankind and the Eucharist, is where catholic truth is found, so that our proper *sitz-im-leben* is the life of grace in which we as catholic persons need to grow to the full potential of our humanity. Salvation then becomes, not the return journey of the individual soul to its Maker, but the catholic process, the gradual unfolding of a universal transfiguration in which men are saved, not from the world, but with the world through the Church.

Our Method

> They set out... as far as the valley of Eshcol, which they explored. They took samples of the fruit of the country and brought them back to us.[1]

In this spirit let our method be to explore the Tradition and to bring back things old and new, things which have been lost or become obscured. The Fathers remain an authoritative reference point for the Church even though today they may be ignored or despised. While recognizing that they require interpretation and need to be brought into a dialectic with modern thought, our concern should be the recovery of *the patristic mind*, the *ekklesiastikon phronema*, a neopatristic synthesis rooted in that central vision of Christian faith— Jesus Christ, Incarnate, Crucified, Risen and Glorified. This will enable the recovery of what was always regarded as integral within Anglican theological method, a concern for Church history and the 'proper', historical setting or context of the Bible—the living apostolic community. It will also ensure, authoritatively, normatively and critically, the historic continuity of the apostolic community and her apostolic faith and praxis. Making this ecclesial dimension the basis of Christian living, and the context of Christian thinking will not add anything to Scripture, but it is the only means to ascertain and to disclose more fully the true meaning of Scripture.

For our hermeneutic let us look to Anglican and other modern prophets, and also to the theologians of Orthodoxy in the West, and to the contribution of the Second Vatican Council on the role of the Church in the modern world.

Our Agenda

With this purpose and method in mind we may pursue the following agenda in our thinking and practice:

1. The rebirth of a living Christian spirituality in which is rediscovered the *sui generis* experience of the Church as the source and datum of theology.

2. In such a spirituality, theology cannot be confined to its contemporary understanding as dialectic argument, rational clarity, and systematic thought. Theology is much more than this contemporary restriction. The enlargement will only come through retrieving the ancient tradition of *theologia*; a *theognosia*—a tradition of wisdom and spirit, or a contemplative theology—in which head and heart are

united, the thirst of the intellect and the drive of the spirit. It is a quest that reaches beyond the intellectual into the realm of imagination, intuition or wholeness.[2]

3. The re-examination of the criteria of theology in the apophatic language of the Fathers, the rediscovery of *the patristic mind*.

4. The rediscovery of *the patristic mind* within the ecclesial context of Anglican divinity.

5. The awakening of the parish as the liturgical community, as the Church in *microcosm* where salvation is known and experienced, recovering such a vision of theology in a contemporary context, bringing such a tradition to life by showing how it continues in our present experience. The only reality that can illuminate our troubled times and give meaning and reality to the irrationality of our confused times is the *One Holy Catholic and Apostolic Church*, the *'little leaven'*.

> Today more than at any other time our personal existence must be anchored in the local parish. The truth of the Church, the reality of salvation, the abolishment of sin and death, the victory over the irrational in life and history— all these for Orthodox derive from the local parish, the actualization of the Body of Christ and the Kingdom of the Father, the Son and the Holy Spirit. The liturgical unity of the faithful has to be the starting point of all things for which we hope: the transformation of the impersonal life of the masses into a communion of persons, the authentic and genuine (rather than the merely theoretical and legal observance of social justice and the deliverance of work from the bondage of mere need and its transformation into an engagement of personal involvement and fellowship. Only the life of the parish can give a priestly dimension to politics, a prophetic spirit to science, a philanthropic concern to economics, a sacramental character to love. Apart from the local parish all these are but an abstraction, naïve idealism, sentimental utopianism. But within the parish there is historical actualization, realistic hope, dynamic manifestation.[3]

6. To search for answers to the problems and questions of modern man in the Holy Tradition, that continuity of life mystical and sacramental that will provide the desperately needed antidotes to the variety of poisons stifling contemporary western life. Such poisons include fragmentation, dehumanization, uncontrolled technology, the loss of nature and the natural world, the War Machine, violence, vandalism, racism, materialism, physical and spiritual poverty.

Conclusion

In the spirit of John Henry Newman, the aim is not the seeking of our own well-being, or originality, or some new invention for the Church. Let our prayer be that God will give us sound judgement, patient thought, discrimination, a comprehensive mind, and abstinence from all private fancies and caprices and personal tastes.[4] Let us seek only the standards of saintliness and service as the measure of our activities.

Notes

1. *Deuteronomy 1:24–25.*
2. Anne E. Carr, *A Search for Wisdom and the Spirit* (Notre Dame 1988), Introduction.
3. C. Yannaras, *Orthodoxy in the West* (ed. A.J. Phillipou), p. 145.
4. J.H. Newman, *Apologia,* p. 82.